ANDREWS, VAN LEEUWEN & VAN BAAREN

HIDDEN PERSUASION

**33 PSYCHOLOGICAL INFLUENCE TECHNIQUES
IN ADVERTISING**

B/S

BIS Publishers
Borneostraat 80-A
1094 CP AMSTERDAM
The Netherlands

-

T +31 (0)20 515 02 30
bis@www.bispublishers.com
www.bispublishers.com

-

Design
andrews:degen,
Amsterdam
Cover Photo
Ralf Mitsch
Text Editing
Bernice Plant

Paperback edition
2nd printing 2023

-

ISBN 9789063695316

-

Copyright © 2013
Marc Andrews, Dr. van Leeuwen,
Prof. Dr. van Baaren and BIS Publishers.

-

Dedicated to you,
the consumer

Advertising is omnipresent in our daily lives. We are exposed to hundreds or even thousands of visual persuasive messages each day. Constantly, these messages attempt to persuade us to feel, believe, act, buy, and to change ourselves. These visual messages reach us at all times and in all kinds of private and public settings, offline as well as online. Fortunately, we lack the ability to process all of this information in a conscious way. Still, some of these carefully constructed visual messages succeed in affecting our attitudes and behaviours more than others, most of the time unconsciously. What is their hidden persuasive force?

Why are we influenced to buy one product over another? How are we stimulated to act and live more sustainably? How are we persuaded to adopt healthier lifestyles?

Throughout this book, advertising is analysed beyond the persuasive power of its imagery. We examine the techniques and concepts hidden behind the visual and aesthetic dimensions of advertising. Advertising is decoded from a psychological point of view, unveiling the hidden unconscious codes that influence our daily decisions.

In this book, 33 social influence techniques are presented based on the latest persuasion and compliance research. The techniques range from influence essentials to more obscure and insidious ones. We describe the underlying processes and techniques that guide our decisions, behaviours, and beliefs. By reading this book, the reader will gain deep insights into how visual means are constructed to influence people on an unconscious level. In the world of social influence, there are several, diverse techniques that can steer people in the desired direction. The origins of social influence are mainly from the fields of rhetoric, obedience, and one-on-one sales. Out of that secret garden, we have selected the techniques that form the backbone of successful advertising.

Now, for the first time, there is a publication that presents a clear overview of social influence techniques used in advertising, enriched with many examples and illustrations. The selected commercials and social advertisements illustrate the techniques visually, which helps the reader to understand how these somewhat abstract concepts are applied in visual communications.

This book is designed as an accessible modern reference book for creating and understanding persuasive visual imagery, making this resource available and comprehensible to a wide range of people.

After reading this book, you will look at advertising differently – whether you are a communication professional, an art director, designer, marketer, businessperson, manager, trader, student, or just a consumer like each of us! In the end, we are all persuaders and targets of persuasion.

This book will open your eyes to the tricks of the trade, we guarantee it!

"

The mind is like an iceberg, it floats with only one-seventh of its bulk above water.

SIGMUND FREUD
founding father of psychoanalysis

Three needs

The techniques in this book are based on three classes of our most basic needs. These are the source of our vulnerability to hidden persuasion. When advertisers use imagery and language that taps into these needs, the audience is unable to fully resist the persuasive power of the message.

System needs

Our cognitive system has evolved from the simplest single cell organism to the advanced brain we use today for conscious analyses, language, and self-reflection. Still ingrained in us, however, are hardwired mental shortcuts that trigger behaviours beyond our control – like the fight-or-flight response we experience when seeing a predatory animal heading straight for us. Advertisements that target these automatic processes have their desired effects before the information becomes available for conscious deliberation. This is the most basic and uncontrollable of the three needs.

Social needs

Humans are social animals; we all want to be loved and respected by friends and strangers alike. Critically, in the past, being cast out from the group posed great danger to individuals, and the fear of social exclusion still lingers in modern man. Other people and their opinions, behaviours, and appearances continue to be some of the most important stimuli we process and one of the biggest influences on our own thoughts, motivations, and behaviours. In this highly demanding and informationally overwhelming world – even though we strongly believe ourselves to be free individuals – we look to others for guidance more than ever. As such, advertisers have an easy task of tapping into our needs for social inclusion and conformity.

Self needs

Third are the needs we usually "feel" as being most important: our personal needs. We avoid pain and strive for pleasure; we want wealth, good food, a stable income, and (most of all) safety. Consciously, we try to make the "best" decisions so that our future self will be content and out of (physical and psychological) danger. This last need is catered to by advertisements using techniques that help project an illusion of a safe and sated, worry-free future.

A. Icons
Shows you which of the three needs (self, social, or system) the technique employs.

B. Name and number of technique

How to use

Read from beginning to end, jump from technique to technique, or just explore the ads and their explanatory captions. There is no right or wrong way to do it; just dive in and get surprised! To get you started, here's an overview of what information you can expect to find.

A ☼ 🏿🏿 ႙

B

08

EFFECTIVENESS	X-FACTOR	IMPLEMENTATION
★★★★★	★★★★☆	★★★☆☆

C

GUARANTEES

D

If you are not satisfied with this book, we offer a money-back guarantee!

This one-liner would be a great sales pitch for the book you have in your hands and would make you confident that you have made the right choice. Unfortunately, it is also a lie. We still hope you enjoy the book though!

Guarantees are one of the most straightforward, easy to understand, and strong resistance removing techniques available. They necessarily imply that no matter what the customer does, in the end they cannot lose. Let the importance of this "insurance policy" sink in. At any moment you (the customer) could decide you're not happy with a product, and then you could return it and get your money back. Similarly, you could come back after receiving bad service or poor advice and return things to the status quo. All skepticism in consumers' purchases is based on whether or not it is the right thing to do or to buy. Guarantees remove any doubt or reluctance to make this decision to purchase. Second, they imply that the product or service is of high quality; if it wasn't, the advertiser would not dare to guarantee it! All one needs to do is to identify the problem or the resistance-inducing factor that inhibits a choice, and then guarantee that this will not be a problem. And that's really how simple it is!

The biggest problem about this technique is that companies have to be able to put their money where their mouth is. If a guarantee is promised, but cannot be delivered, the guarantee is a lie and customers will be enraged.

56

F

C. Persuasion factor
In this expert judgment rating, the techniques are scored on the dimensions of: **'Effectiveness'**, **'X-Factor'** and **'Ease of implementation'**. The **Effectiveness factor** indicates the extent to which the technique will affect the viewer/reader. It represents the potency of the technique and the likelihood of it having the desired effect. The **X-Factor** describes the "WOW" element of the technique. How sexy the technique is, including: how innovative it is, how interesting it is from a scientific perspective, and how intriguing its workings are. The **Ease of Implementation factor** indicates how easy or hard it is to apply that scientific technique to advertising in practice. Some very interesting techniques are rarely ever applied or require very specific conditions, whereas others can easily be applied to almost any ad in any setting. Of course the judgment is informed but subjective by nature. Scores range from 1 (low) to 5 (high) stars.

D. The one-liner
A first glance at what the
technique is all about.

E. Ads and illustrations
The techniques are demonstrated using
advertisements from around the world,
putting the more abstract and theoretical ideas presented in text into concrete
visual examples. Note, however, that
a persuasive technique itself can be
part of an overall campaign strategy
and is not limited to individual visual
advertisements. Of course, how easily
a technique can be recognised and how
effectively it can be implemented varies
widely. We do not know the degree to
which these ads were actually constructed around the underlying influence
technique; we only show that they con-
tain them. The images are supported by
descriptions interpreting the use of the
technique. In some cases, techniques
are supported by our own illustrations
instead of existing ads. Image credits
can be found in the back of the book.

This ad visually insinuates a guarantee of everlastingness. On the plus
side, there is no direct claim, and thus no need to follow up on it. On the
other hand, the more explicit, clear, and strong a guarantee is, the better
it works.

FINAL
ARKS
→ A guarantee needs to be demonstrably credible;
  make sure that it can be delivered.
→ Consumers should be aware of complicated return
  policies. A guarantee policy alone is not always a
  reflection of the producer's trust in the quality of the
  product, but this combined with a simple return policy
  is a good sign.

Anticipatory regret, "It's free!" bias,
Post-purchase rationalisation

G. Final remarks
Points out important conclusions
and advice on the technique.

F. Main text
Explains the technique, the circumstances under which it works and
why, as well as the dos and don'ts and
how-to tips for applying the technique.
Scientific sources can be found in the
back of the book. We have also included
a list of other interesting and inspiring
books related to the fields of psychology,
social influence, communication, design,
visual rhetoric, and advertising.

H. Related concepts 🔍
Lists a selection of concepts related
to the technique, useful for further
online exploration.

EFFECTIVENESS | X-FACTOR | IMPLEMENTATION
★ ★ ★ ★ ★ | ★ ★ ★ ★ ★ | ★ ★ ★ ★ ★

ACKNOWLEDGING RESISTANCE

Overcoming resistance by simply acknowledging it

Resistance to influence and persuasion is the single most problematic aspect of getting someone to do or purchase something. It is, therefore, no wonder that most persuaders and requesters do everything they can to avoid emphasising or calling attention to possible negative responses to their request. Paradoxically, research has shown that acknowledging someone's resistance to comply or emphasising that they are free to do as they want removes hesitation, increases liking of the requester, and induces compliance. The most remarkable thing about these two techniques is that they require no additional methods of persuasion to be used, and no extra information needs to be processed. It is as simple as saying, "I know you will not agree to this, but..." before a proposal or adding, "But you are free to accept or refuse" after the proposal. While both techniques play into our tendency to resist influence, there are differences between these approaches.

Acknowledging resistance (AR) necessitates that there be resistance to the upcoming proposal in advance, as would be expected when raising taxes or fees on a service. It plays into this existing resistance by simply acknowledging its presence. It not only eliminates the possibility of the target using the argument, "But I don't want to," but also communicates an empathic understanding of that person's opinion.

Hans Brinker acknowledges that budget is budget by embracing "cheap" instead of trying to camouflage it. No luxury (images above), only the basics (next page) and no extensive service (page 18). In these series of ads, acknowledging resistance is combined with an element of humour and surprise. The take-home message "...but we are very affordable" is not explicitly stated, but left to be discovered by the viewer once he/she has understood the ad.

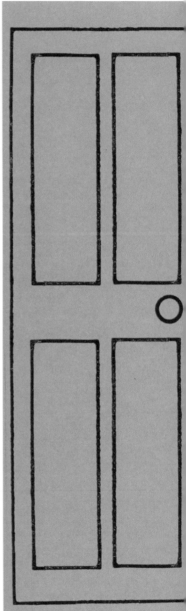

NOW
A DOOR
N EVERY
ROOM !

Hans Brinker
Budget Hotel
Amsterdam
☎ 31 20 6220687

NOW:~
FREE KEY
WITH YOUR
ROOM

Hans Brinker
Budget Hotel
Amsterdam
☎ 31 20 6220687

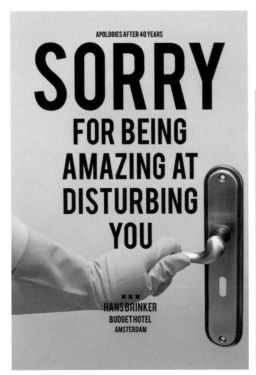

Importantly, the acknowledgement must be at the beginning of the sentence or proposal. In a few cases, the technique can be used as an attempt at reverse psychology: Telling the target what they do not want, paradoxically, makes them want exactly this.

The but you are free (BYAF) technique is hot off the press! It was first reported by Guegguen and Pascal in 2000, and a large review of 42 studies on its effectiveness appeared in 2013. This review showed that emphasising that people are free to choose at the end of a proposal doubled the overall compliance with a direct request. While AR works because the initial answer would be "No," BYAF makes no assumption about the original attitude. Instead, it generates and enhances a sense of freedom by allowing a "No" response. This makes the BYAF technique slightly more versatile and less prone to reactance.

The specific wording of the AR and BYAF techniques is not that important, as long as there is an acknowledgement of resistance or an emphasis on freedom, respectively. Again, both techniques work, paradoxically,

by highlighting the target's autonomy to say "No" and they have the
added benefit of making the requester appear respectful of the target's
choice. Both work best for face-to-face requests or in situations where the
target is not anonymous – anonymity removes the need for self-presenta-
tion (and therefore resistance) because the request can be dismissed easily.
Thus, the requester should be able to see whether the target follows up
on the request. The two main benefits of these techniques are their
non-reliance on the content of the proposal and their ease of use.
By adding a few simple words to the beginning or the end of a request
compliance can be significantly increased.

**FINAL
REMARKS**
→ Especially effective when the target feels he or she
   ought to comply with the proposal morally, but does
   not really want to or is avoiding it (e.g., campaigns
   promoting safe sex or donations).
→ BYAF is suitable for almost any request, and both AR
   and BYAF can be used easily in combination with other
   influence techniques.
→ The effect is strongest when the target is not
   anonymous.

🔎 **Reverse psychology, Transparency**

EFFECTIVENESS | X-FACTOR | IMPLEMENTATION
★ ★ ★ ★ ★ | ★ ★ ★ ★ ★ | ★ ★ ★ ★ ★

FLUENCY

A message should always be experienced fluently and with ease

A lot of people think that using difficult words and sentences make them look smart. The opposite is true; it actually makes you look less intelligent. This effect is not due to our sharp skills in detecting when someone is a poseur, but simply because human brains do not like complexity. Keep it simple, stupid!

Smooth and automatic processing of information automatically leads to experiencing positive feelings. This works for visual, textual, and conceptual information alike. The quicker something is read, the easier an image is on the eye, and/or the faster a concept is understood, the more we will like it. Thus, choosing the right name, font, number, and image can make all the difference in whether a message will have any persuasive impact.

Naming

In naming, the choice of pronounceable vs. unpronounceable names determines whether people find your product safe or threatening, boring or exciting. Researchers have found that when people were confronted with medicine names like Magnalroxate and Hnegripitrom the latter was reported as more threatening. This effect can, however, be used to your advantage. When naming theme park rides, researchers found that rides with unpronounceable Indian names (e.g., Tsiischili) were experienced as more exciting and sickening than ones with pronounceable names (e.g., Chunta). Thus, if you are selling a product designed to induce feelings of safety and familiarity, go for flow. If, on the other hand, you are selling something exciting or extravagant, you could name it Rhrtixtrax.

Numbering

The way products are numbered can also increase fluency. You may have already noticed that many well-known brands incorporate numbers in their product line, such as Nikon D40 / D50 and BMW 1- / 3- / 5- series. These numbers not only help to distinguish one product from another, but can also increase product preference when chosen wisely. For example, an imaginary product would likely be evaluated as more desirable if named "Zinc 24" than if it was just called "Zinc."

An example of an extremely brain friendly number combination. Not only are the numbers very familiar, but they are also even. Furthermore, 8 is two times 4, and the numeric increases from 0 to 4 and 4 to 8 are the same, thereby making the numbers reinforce each other.

But why 24 and not 23? An interesting set of studies has explored which numbers are evaluated more positively than others. The research demonstrated that well-known (and therefore fluently processed) numbers in ads increased the positive evaluation of the product itself. Additionally, if the mathematical product of two displayed numbers was included, evaluations were even higher. For example, people were asked to make a choice between V8 and Campbell's soup. Some were told: "Get a full day's supply of 4 essential vitamins and 2 minerals with a bottle of V8," whereas others saw an advertisement that stated: "Get a full day's supply of essential vitamins and minerals with a bottle of V8." More people chose V8 when the numbers 2 and 4 were included. The number 8 is not only familiar and easily divisible, but also $2 \times 4 = 8$ making for an even more fluent processing of the message. The operands 2 and 4 then help the unconscious processing of the number 8. The researchers suggest that this only works for simple multiplications, as most of us have learned these by heart and are quick to recognise them.

Typeface
Fonts influence how easy it is to read a given text. As expected, the less readable the font, the less we like it. For example, one study found that when exercise instructions were written using a font that was difficult to read, participants thought that the exercise would take twice as long to complete and expected it to be more demanding. Of course this effect can also be used to our advantage. Presenting Japanese spring rolls on a menu using a font that was hard to read made people rate the dish as more complex (therefore superior). But unless you are an aspiring Michelin chef or selling advanced electronics it is better to avoid using the "wing dings" font.

Now try to answer the following question, "How many animals of each kind did Moses take on the ark?" Most people respond with "Two" despite their knowledge that Moses never had an ark. When this sentence was written using a font that was more difficult to read, however, the percentage of readers detecting the trick question went from 17% to 41%. So, under certain circumstances, decreasing the fluency of text can jolt people into

A rare example where lower fluency (or processing ease) fits with the message. Jazz is traditionally associated with complexity and creativity. It is not supposed to be consumed easily. Additionally, the main purpose of the text in these ads is not to convey a lot of information, but to create an atmosphere.

a more analytical processing mode. This is useful when you want people to consider the message carefully, and you are confident that it will hold up to scrutiny.

The effect of fluency does not only work on a perceptual level. When we find an action easy to imagine we like it more and are more likely to perform it later. In a similar vein, if you show someone a scene that they could easily imagine themselves in (e.g., a beach from a first-person viewpoint), they are more likely to want to go there than to a scene that is harder to imagine (e.g., the same beach from an aerial viewpoint). Even more surprising, studies have shown that if you ask someone to imagine a positive product experience this actually has a positive impact on their product evaluations later, but only if the product itself was accompanied by vivid imagery. One can further facilitate imagery fluency by combi-ning images that support each other. For example, a picture of a lock is reported as more beautiful when preceded by an image of a key. In sum, it is not only the perceptual properties of text or images that are important, but also the ease with which something can be brought to mind.

Using traffic related material in a novel way to construct a message can lead to heightened interest and increased attention. However, merging imagery and words often leads to greater difficulties in reading, and thus in slower processing of the message. Low fluency can also make people stop reading the message half way through due to time constraints.

Overall, fluent processing is most effective when people process the information quickly and heuristically. In other words, fluency is good if your
visual message relates to something that people do not need to pay much
attention to or if you specifically want your target to remain in a peripheral
processing mode. However, if you want to jolt people into carefully considering your message, you can do this by including a word that is difficult
to pronounce or surprising imagery. Note that in most cases, however,
an audience does not have the conscious capacity or the time to carefully
consider presented messages. Therefore, familiar and fluent messages
are an advertiser's safest bet.

To conclude, people are highly sensitive to experiences of ease and
difficulty, but are not aware of how this influences them. They tend to
attribute any resulting positive and negative evaluations to other properties of the textual or visual material (e.g., they believe that they make their
decisions based on the content) and will not recognise that understanding
something with ease automatically induces positive affect.

**FINAL
REMARKS**

→ A message should be clean, simple, and perceptually
pleasing. All fluent processing is experienced as positive
affect, which is then transferred to the message and/or
source.
→ Complicated messages are to be avoided, as they result
in the audience perceiving the source as less intelligent
or the message as less appealing.
→ If a product or message is all about sophistication and
complexity, induce disfluency by using difficult fonts
and confusing imagery.
→ Get people to read a message more carefully by using
a font that is difficult to read (Caution: it could cause
people to ignore the message altogether).

⊘ **Ease of retrieval, Framing, Hot-cold empathy gap,
Regulatory fit**

EFFECTIVENESS	X-FACTOR	IMPLEMENTATION
★ ★ ★ ★ ★	★ ★ ★ ★ ★	★ ★ ★ ★ ★

FOOT-IN-THE-DOOR

Beginning with a small request paves the way for compliance to a bigger request

Imagine that someone asks you to donate a small amount of money to support volunteer work with the elderly, and you agree. A week later that same person approaches you and asks if you are willing to spend an hour at the local nursing home to interact with the residents, and you agree again. This is a successful instance of the foot-in-the-door technique (FITD).

FITD is a multiple-step influence strategy. First you ask people to comply with a seemingly small request. A short while afterwards, you ask them a bigger request, which is in line with the smaller one. It turns out that starting with a small request strongly increases the chances of complying with the big request compared to only asking the big request.

The exact psychological mechanism underlying FITD remains subject to debate. Most likely, several psychological processes account for its effect. The first explanation is self-perception, which means that you observe your behaviour (agreeing to donate) and then adjust your attitude to the behaviour (I must find that important/noble/good, etc.). Because you changed your attitude, the next request is in line with your newly adopted attitude. Other explanations centre round the themes of commitment and /or consistency. The idea is that you made a public commitment to a cause by agreeing to the first request and you don't want to appear inconsistent and unreliable by not agreeing to the second request.

The use of in-app purchases is gaining ground as a new way to implement the foot-in-the-door technique. Instead of asking for a product's full price up front, it is initially marketed as "free." Then, while using the app, it is possible to buy additional desirable functionality. This is particularly effective for games: By making the buying threshold low, and having people spend time and effort using the app, it is an easy way to make customers want more. Note: If the "free" claim is a lie, however, and people are prompted to pay when opening the app, it is a form of the foot-in-the door technique known as the low-ball technique (see related concepts).

DRIVE SLOW!
DRIVE SAFE!

DRIVE SLOW! DRIVE SAFE!

Researchers going door-to-door first asked random households to put a sticker in their window to promote safe driving. A small request, and almost everyone agreed. A while later the researchers returned, asking them to put a large and rather unsightly sign in their yard that also promoted safe driving. Of the people who were first approached with the small favour, 76% agreed to display the sign in their yard; however, of those not approached with the first request, only 17% agreed.

This effect will be even stronger when the first and second requests are made by the same person, as they know about your initial agreement.

The FITD has been studied widely in the lab and has been used abundantly in real-life situations. It is one of the most famous influence techniques and one with a high success rate when performed correctly. The FITD is most effective when, among other things:

+ The first request involves some level of effort and is an actual behaviour; not just a simple "Yes."
+ People get complimented or receive recognition for taking the first step.
+ The bigger request is clearly related to and in line with the first request.

Despite its strong effects when used correctly, there are several aspects of the FITD technique that can decrease its effectiveness. First, it may lead to resistance. When the same person approaches you twice, it may feel pushy or aggressive and lead to reactance. Second, the first request needs to be large enough that it requires action from the target, but it should not be too large or you'll get a "No." Obviously, the FITD only works when the first, smaller, request receives a "Yes."

FINAL REMARKS

→ Asking for a big favour at once often leads to resistance; starting with a small, related request greatly increases the success rate.

→ The first request should neither be too small (it needs to be high in involvement) nor too big.

🔎 **Rationalisation trap, Bait-and-switch, Ben Franklin effect, Low-ball Technique**

| EFFECTIVENESS | X-FACTOR | IMPLEMENTATION |
| ★ ★ ★ ★ ★ | ★ ★ ★ ★ ★ | ★ ★ ★ ★ ★ |

PROMISED LAND

Buy this product
and follow me to the Promised Land

Normally, consumers buy products because they fulfil their basic needs (e.g., hunger, cleanliness). However, product-irrelevant needs (social, emotional, and sexual) can also be promised for purchasing a basic need product. The Promised Land is a persuasion technique which seduces consumers into buying a product because it will help them to achieve some desirable goal – even when the goal is unrealistic.

This technique is opposite to those where the audience is persuaded to buy a product on the basis of concrete and "honest" attributes (rationally). The Promised Land is directly aimed at creating the strongest reward response in the brain of the perceiver. Even though the claims made are exaggerated or obvious lies, they target the important desires we carry with us, thereby making us vulnerable to them.

This can happen in at least two ways:

1. People want the exaggerated claims to be true. We may convince ourselves that even though we will, of course, not attract a horde of sexy models; we will at least get more attention from attractive women when we use a sexualised product like Axe deodorants (see next page).

In many ways, Axe's campaign is the essence of seduction. The partly explicit, partly implicit claims by Axe are over the top. However, their exaggerations are presented in a funny and self-ironic way, so we gladly accept them without resistance. Additionally, we feel attracted to the product by seeing these fantasies come true, and we (un)consciously associate the ad with our own interpersonal romantic situations and aspirations.

2. By presenting these brands with very attractive, but unrealistic situations, the ads create an association between our dreams and desires and the specific brand. When a teenage male goes out to a bar, attracting women is likely to be a motive, and the teenager most likely has some hopes and fantasies in that department. When he is in that frame of mind, liquor ads associated with sex are likely to come to his mind, since liquor has been linked to that goal previously.

The Promised Land can be seen as an empowering promise; it will give you the right tools and powers to succeed. It is not so much about actual empowerment ("You will absolutely succeed when you buy this"), but about increasing the target's self-esteem ("I feel a (little) more confident now that I will attract these desirable women"). A straightforward example regarding the empowerment aspect of the promise is the iconic slogan by Nike, "Just do it!" It implies that you will succeed. It gives you some trust that wearing Nike products will make you a better athlete, and thus help you to reach your athletic goals.

Promised Lands are used widely in many domains (perfumes, cars, athletics, detergents, etc.). The most interesting aspect of the technique is the fact that we know it is not (completely) true, but we wish it to be true – emotionally, we feel inspired and attracted to it. Thus, the Promised Land is the epitome of advertising as a way of luring and seducing the public.

FINAL REMARKS
→ The Promised Land inspires people, even when they know that the promise is exaggerated or unrealistic.
→ Even unachievable desires are strong motivators for human behaviour.

🔍 **Empowerment, Framing, Psychological transportation**

The ads suggest that there are fragrances which make the other sex go crazy and forget about the world around them to focus on wanting you. Although not explicitly stated, this is a gross exaggeration of what pheromones do in nature. In many species (likely also in humans), there are scents that activate the "reproductive urge" in the brain. Maybe this phenomenon is part of the success of Axe: what if they're right?

EFFECTIVENESS | X-FACTOR | IMPLEMENTATION
★ ★ ★ ★ ★ | ★ ★ ★ ★ ★ | ★ ★ ★ ☆ ☆

SELF-PERSUASION

No one is better than you at persuading yourself to change

The biggest problem in persuasion is overcoming a target's resistance to influence by another. This is especially true when significant changes in behaviour are required. Trying to persuade someone to stop smoking, to start donating, to volunteer to help at a children's hospital, or to practise safe sex, requires quite different techniques from, say, trying to persuade someone to grab a Dr. Pepper instead of a Coke when they are thirsty. While the latter can be achieved using subtle and unconscious influence techniques that nudge the behaviour in the desired direction, achieving the former effectively and permanently is one of societies' and advertisers' greatest challenges. People do not like to be told how to live or what alliances to choose; people like to believe they are in control of making the major decisions in their lives.

Playing into this freedom perspective, an extensive line of research has demonstrated that when an influence attempt is felt as being generated from within the target, their internal defenses are almost completely surpassed. If people feel that they have provided the positive arguments for performing a certain action themselves, they're much more likely to believe these arguments and to behave accordingly. The resulting be-haviour follows the belief, as one of the main human drives is to be and feel (or at least to appear) outwardly consistent. This need for consistency

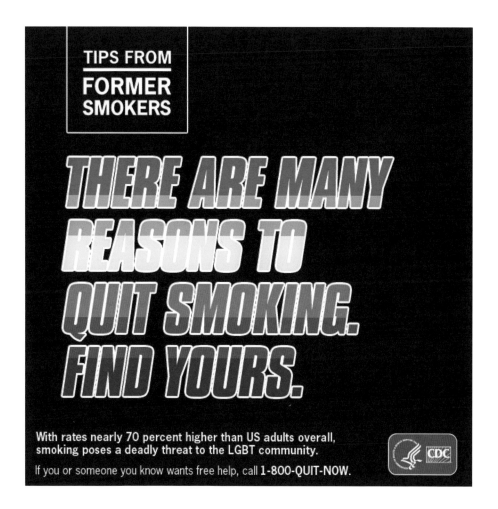

With rates nearly 70 percent higher than US adults overall, smoking poses a deadly threat to the LGBT community.

If you or someone you know wants free help, call 1-800-QUIT-NOW.

A reader who takes some time to digest this ad is stimulated to think of reasons not to smoke. He/she will then come up with intrinsic reasons resulting in almost no resistance to the message (why argue with yourself?!). If the ad had given some reasons in the text, the first reaction would have been to evaluate them and look for flaws. By using self-persuasion, this does not happen. The challenge of course is to make sure people will actually take the time to generate reasons. Finally, "tips from former smokers" conveys both similarity (smokers don't like to listen to non-smokers, but former smokers are considered part of the in-group) and self-efficacy (they are like me, and they were able to quit, so I can quit too!).

means that when people are asked to advocate a position (e.g., in favour of raising taxes), they subsequently agree more with this position – even if they do not initially support it themselves. This is known as counter-attitudinal advocacy.

Self-persuasion (SP) has repeatedly been demonstrated to trump any kind of given high-quality argument. A good example is taken from re-search into persuasive anti-smoking messages. Researchers had smokers either write down a few arguments about why smoking is bad (SP) or pro-vided them with strong arguments about why smoking is bad. Afterwards, participants who generated their own reasons were only half as likely to light up a cigarette. A follow-up experiment replicated these effects by only showing people the question "Why is smoking bad?" Asking this question resulted in smokers generating counter-smoking arguments in their minds and behaving accordingly. Similar experiments on helping behaviour have shown 90% increases in agreeing to help when applying SP (i.e., writing down two arguments about why helping is good). The best effect for the provided arguments was 60% and was only achieved by providing ten high-quality arguments.

HOW WILL YOU SPEND
YOUR LAST 10 YEARS?
The average Canadian will spend
their last ten years in sickness.
Change your future now.

MAKE
HEALTH
LAST.CA

HEART &
STROKE
FOUNDATION

The campaign uses a guided or suggestive type of self-persuasion, which comes close to a rhetorical question. If there were no images presented with the question, people would be able to think of any answer. With the image, there is an implicit choice between "sick" and "enjoying life". This question stimulates you to choose between the two implicit options, and you will always choose "enjoying life". The next step in this effective chain of influence is then to ask "how do I stay healthy for those last 10 years?" The answer to that question is given in the finer print: "Change your future now" implies you will find the answer at the Heart & Stroke Foundation. It would have been an option to include a call to action in that final part, so not just change your future now, but a donation request, visit the website or a suggestion for healthy behaviour, but it still is a beautifully constructed ad.

HOW WILL YOU SPEND YOUR LAST 10 YEARS?

The average Canadian will spend their last ten years in sickness. Change your future now.

MAKE HEALTH LAST.CA

 HEART &™ STROKE FOUNDATION

This technique is, to some extent, the "holy grail" of persuasion research. First, targets persuade themselves, thereby minimising effort for the persuader. Second, there is no confrontation or resistance, and behavioural change is long-term and stable, as the generated arguments turn into personal beliefs (e.g., I am a loyal Apple user). The challenge in applying this technique, of course, is to get people in the right state of mind to self-generate these arguments. It is not enough to frame messages as questions; people need the motivation, ability, and time to process these messages before mentally generating their arguments. Therefore, unless the question stands out from the clutter and will definitely engage the mind, it is advisable to have people physically write down or orally present the arguments.

FINAL REMARKS

→ SP effects increase significantly when people make their self-generated statements publicly, when they are taped or filmed, and when their arguments are written down.

→ People need to feel personally responsible for the arguments in order for SP to work. If external pressure is too high (e.g. they feel forced to generate the arguments, or are paid a lot of money to do it), people will attribute the arguments to external sources, and thus increase their resistance.

→ SP combines particularly well with implementation intentions.

→ Less is more for SP: generating two arguments works better than 10.

🔎 **Counter-attitudinal advocacy, Insufficient justification, Rationalisation trap**

06

EFFECTIVENESS	X-FACTOR	IMPLEMENTATION
★ ★ ★ ★ ★	★ ★ ★ ★ ☆	★ ★ ★ ★ ☆

ALTERCASTING

Casting people into a social role
makes them behave in ways expected by this role

In its simplest form, altercasting is telling someone that they are "good" and that they should behave accordingly: "John, you are an intelligent and conscientious person; I know you will work hard at finishing this task on time." Wanting indeed to be seen as an intelligent and conscientious person, this traps John to perform the behaviour expected by such a person.

There are two types of altercasting: manded and tact. Manded altercasting is when a person is placed in a social position orally or textually: "John, as a true American, you should…" Tact altercasting, a more subtle approach, is often created with suggestive imagery to have someone take on the role spontaneously and voluntarily. For example, including a child in a road safety campaign makes the viewer take on the role of protector by awakening feelings of responsibility for the safety of the child. These particularly forceful social techniques are based on the assumption that when someone accepts a social position – such as an expert, trustee, helper, protector, friend, or patriot – subsequent information-seeking and behaviour is informed by this new identity.

Altercasting (manded and tact) is used widely in our daily conversations and is a recurring theme in visual media – most often in health and other social marketing campaigns. It is also used by large corporations casting

Men often want to be seen in the aspired social role of the strong and sturdy guy. This campaign tries to activate the classic male role of the hunter and adventurer. To meet and fulfil this role, and to behave consistently with the presented image, men should feel stimulated to use the product in question. Lait d'homme emphasises the man as a hunter in a funny and exaggerated way. The textual information explicitly underscores and activates the social role of being a man: "Lait d'homme - The manly chocolate milk for men with added man," making this an example of manded alter-casting. If you are a tough man or you see yourself as one, you'd better drink this chocolate milk! This is an interesting attempt at infusing a product that's traditionally not very manly with machismo, thereby reaching a new demographic.

LAIT
D'HOMME

THE MANLY CHOCOLATE MILK FOR MEN WITH ADDED MAN

Zo.
Nu
eerst
een
Bavaria

Bavaria uses a more subtle form of altercasting, known as tact altercasting. It shows an adventurous guy enjoying his Bavarian beer after surviving dangerous encounters with wildlife, without explicitly emphasising the role with words.

Zo.
Nu
eerst
een
Bavaria

themselves into protective roles (e.g., oil companies) and by consumer goods companies having buyers take on their brand "naturally" as an identity (e.g., Apple). The high prevalence of this technique is due to its ease of application: It takes only a few words or a simple image to conjure up the corresponding social role in the mind of the receiver. Additionally, it evokes minimal resistance to influence (especially in the case of tact altercasting), as the role adaptation comes from within the receiver and not from an external source. A final benefit is that the number of ways in which altercasting can be applied is only limited by the number of social roles that exist, which is virtually limitless!

FINAL REMARKS

→ The easiest and most effective way to cast someone into a social role is verbally (e.g., "You as an expert should..."); however, it also works using written messages. This is manded altercasting.

→ An image can portray someone in a particular social role (e.g., a baby in a nuclear disarmament campaign) to encourage the recipient to naturally take on the counter role (e.g., the responsible protector). This is tact altercasting.

🔎 **Hypnosis, Injunctive norms, Role-play**

In this campaign, Delas activates the role of "businesswoman" and "leader" in women. Women are known to have to struggle with a multitude of roles (good businesswoman, good mother, sexy lover, interested friend, etc.). Delas tries to make women see that they, too, can achieve whatever they want in life. Women, it's not just for men... activate the businesstiger within you!

POR QUE NÃO?

EFFECTIVENESS	X-FACTOR	IMPLEMENTATION
★ ★ ★ ★ ★	★ ★ ★ ★ ☆	★ ★ ★ ★ ☆

SOCIAL PROOF

People have an innate drive to copy others' decisions and behaviour

Modern-day Western culture is extraordinarily individualistic. We believe that our actions are our own and that our decisions are driven by private needs. However, humans are social animals: Across the ages we have depended on groups to survive, and other people's behaviour is highly informative for successfully choosing our own course of action. Given this firmly held belief that we are our own masters, it may seem paradoxical that social proof is particularly powerful as an influence technique. However, it is due to this belief that we are less prepared to defend ourselves against social pressures.

How does social proof work in advertising? Surprisingly, one of the easiest and most effective ways to use this technique is by simply stating that "90% of X do/buy/prefer Y." Where X is your target's social group and Y is the behaviour they show or the product they buy. This should be preceded or followed by a positive message about the product. While sounding childishly simple and transparent, this and similar phrasing has been shown to strongly influence consumer behaviour, time and time again. Alternatively, percentages can be substituted by "Nearly (or almost) everyone" or "The majority of people." It is equally easy to demonstrate visually by showing the relevant group performing the action or purchasing the product of interest. Such visual demonstrations have the added benefit of being less explicit, and thus less confronting than a direct statement.

Opinions from others who are similar to you are especially valuable. If you are an Elvis fan, and all other Elvis fans think this is the best CD, who are you to argue? And just in case you were unsure, dozens of Elvises on the cover convince you that there is a whole lot of him on this LP.

Especially when enquiring about a product's quality, nothing works better than hearing from others that they approve of it. It is obvious that products which have the highest star ratings (i.e., up to five stars) and the greatest number of positive appraisals sell the most. These days, it is even possible to buy Facebook 'likes' and positive book or restaurant reviews, as retailers employ the power of social proof (SEE ASTROTURFING, PAGE 99). It is therefore important for any service provider to clearly display information about client and customer satisfaction.

When more people approve of something, we're more likely to like it too.The impact of social proof is exponential; with increasing numbers of people liking something, it is also increasingly likely that other people will press 'like', resulting in more people liking it.

563 people like it

98

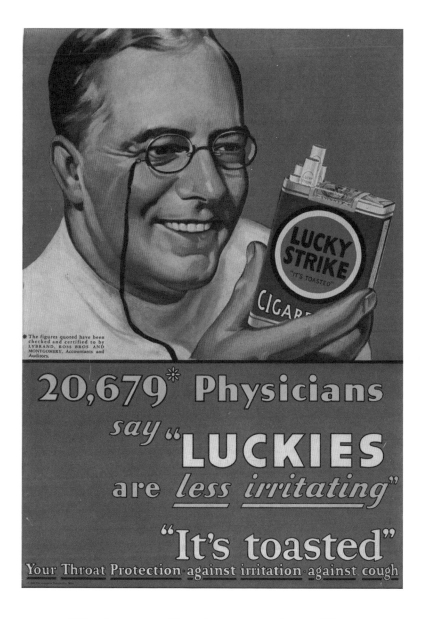

This advertisement includes an interesting combination of social proof and authority (SEE AUTHORITY, PAGE 145). Not only do these doctors know what they are talking about, but they all seem to agree with each other! Or do you think that you know better than 20,679 physicians? Note the use of an exact number after the comma, which makes the number seem genuine. Obviously, social proof only works if the audience believes that theopinions are from real people.

If the number of endorsers is perceived as lower than the expected number or than that displayed by similar products, the effect reverses and using this technique becomes disadvantageous. Perhaps less obvious, extreme caution is necessary when using social proof to ensure that the "wrong" behaviour is not highlighted. Often government campaigns draw attention to problem behaviours by stating, "90% of people do X. Don't do X!" Where X is a dangerous or unhealthy, or a socially unacceptable behaviour (e.g., stealing, smoking, swearing, drunk-driving, etc.). Research shows that this strategy makes people perform these undesirable behaviours more because they see it as the norm. Thus, it appears that regardless of the target behaviour, one of the easiest and most foolproof shortcuts people use when making decisions continues to be looking at what others do.

FINAL REMARKS

→ Social proof works especially well when it is not clear what the correct decision or behaviour is in a specific situation (e.g., impulse buying).

→ While people are sensitive to any majority opinion, groups that are similar or physically close have the greatest impact.

→ Young people are particularly sensitive to the effects of social proof.

○ **Asch Line Length experiments, Autokinetic effect, Bandwagon effect, Bystander effect, Copycat suicides, Information cascade**

Have you also noticed so many Hyundais lately?

This is a combination of social evidential value, self-persuasion (SEE PAGE 36) and mere exposure (SEE PAGE 90). The descriptive norm is activated by the word 'also' (apparently there are many others who have also noticed it), and creates the impression that there are lots of Hyundais riding around. By putting this as a question instead of as a statement, it removes resistance and causes people to cast their minds back to the question every time they see a Hyundai. The brilliant thing is that it is a self-confirming message: every time you see a Hyundai, you think: there goes another one again, while you never noticed them before. Owing to the repeated exposure (the mere exposure effect), every observation reinforces people becoming more positive about Hyundai.

"

Half the money
I spend on
advertising is
wasted, and the
problem is I don't
know which half.

JOHN WANAMAKER
marketing pioneer

EFFECTIVENESS | X-FACTOR | IMPLEMENTATION
★★★★★ | ★★★★☆ | ★★★☆☆

GUARANTEES

If you are not satisfied with this book, we offer a money-back guarantee!

This one-liner would be a great sales pitch for the book you have in your hands and would make you confident that you have made the right choice. Unfortunately, it is also a lie. We still hope you enjoy the book though!

Guarantees are one of the most straightforward, easy to understand, and strong resistance removing techniques available. They necessarily imply that no matter what the customer does, in the end they cannot lose. Let the importance of this "insurance policy" sink in. At any moment you (the customer) could decide you're not happy with a product, and then you could return it and get your money back. Similarly, you could come back after receiving bad service or poor advice and return things to the status quo. All skepticism in consumers' purchases is based on whether or not it is the right thing to do or to buy. Guarantees remove any doubt or reluctance to make this decision to purchase. Second, they imply that the product or service is of high quality; if it wasn't, the advertiser would not dare to guarantee it! All one needs to do is to identify the problem or the resistance-inducing factor that inhibits a choice, and then guarantee that this will not be a problem. And that's really how simple it is!

The biggest problem about this technique is that companies have to be able to put their money where their mouth is. If a guarantee is promised, but cannot be delivered, the guarantee is a lie and customers will be enraged.

VOTRE MATÉRIEL RESTE COMME NEUF
3 ANS DE GARANTIE

VOTRE MATÉRIEL RESTE COMME NEUF
3 ANS DE GARANTIE

This is a classic example of the guarantee technique, where Stihl guarantees their equipment for three years. The message clearly conveys that for all practical purposes buyers will be working with a brand-new product for that period. In other words: if it works as new, no problem; if it breaks it is repaired to function as new; and if repair is not possible, you will get a new one. In any case: it's as good as new.

Speak for yourself.
Anonymity guaranteed.

NEWFOUNDLAND
LABRADOR
LIQUOR CORPORATION

HELLO

Speak
&Spell

Use your real voice.
Anonymity guaranteed.

NEWFOUNDLAND
LABRADOR
LIQUOR CORPORATION

Guarantees are not limited to product warranties.
Guarantees can also be used to remove doubts
about any behaviour, providing they are true and
believable. In the case of reporting crime, it is
known that the fear of retaliation or of being
approached by the police is the largest hurdle.

Companies have dodged this problem by making use of the guarantee excruciatingly hard for customers. This way they can still advertise the guarantee (because it is theoretically true), while making sure that of the customers who are unhappy with their product, very few will return it.

The classic example of this is the devious sale of polished wooden knobs as vibrators. In this scheme, ads promoted the world's best vibrator in existence, claiming: "If this vibrator does not get you off, nothing will," along with: "All this for the low price of €20." And the best was yet to come, with a: "Not satisfied? Full money-back guarantee!" statement. Normally such a claim, and price, would raise suspicion, but with a full guarantee what could possibly go wrong? If the product wasn't what was expected, it could be returned. As a consequence, it sold in the thousands. However, when opening the package, people found it contained only a short wooden dildo. Infuriated, customers looked through the guarantee policy and procedure. To get their money back, they had to deliver the package to the post office, clearly stating "Arse Ticklers Faggots Fanclub" on the top of the package, with their return address on the back. Unsurprisingly, very few returns were made – who would dare to look the post office clerk in the eyes?! The clever part here was that there were no lies. There was a guarantee, and those customers who returned the product did get their money back. But enormous profits were made by making the process of returning the product so difficult. Interestingly, the company was later sued for false advertising (but not due to their guarantee statement!).

Another, much less sinister, example of a success story of applying guarantees is Walmart's "satisfaction guaranteed" policy. A 90-day return period in combination with no need for a receipt is a textbook application of this technique. The effectiveness of this technique is in the knowledge that humans are a lazy species. That is, even when it is very easy for us to return something, a great number of us often don't bother or forget to do so.

This ad visually insinuates a guarantee of everlastingness. On the plus side, there is no direct claim, and thus no need to follow up on it. On the other hand, the more explicit, clear, and strong a guarantee is, the better it works.

FINAL REMARKS

→ A guarantee needs to be demonstrably credible; make sure that it can be delivered.

→ Consumers should be aware of complicated return policies. A guarantee policy alone is not always a reflection of the producer's trust in the quality of the product, but this combined with a simple return policy is a good sign.

🔍 **Anticipatory regret, "It's free!" bias, Post-purchase rationalisation**

EFFECTIVENESS	X-FACTOR	IMPLEMENTATION
★ ★ ★ ★ ☆	★ ★ ★ ★ ☆	★ ★ ★ ★ ★

ATTRACTIVENESS

> "It is amazing how complete is the delusion
> that beauty is goodness."
> **Leo Tolstoy, The Kreutzer Sonata**

In our culture, striving for equality, we have decided that children should be brought up with maxims illustrating the shallowness of beauty, such as: "Beauty is only skin-deep" and "Beauty is in the eye of the beholder." Given this, it seems paradoxical that societies – Western societies in particular – abound in the use of attractiveness in ad placements, magazines, films, and all other visual media. A natural consequence of this bombardment is that people are continuously surrounded by the attractiveness ideal while simultaneously being expected not to judge a book by its cover.

And people really do believe that they are not seduced more by beautiful men and women in ads toting a company's product. However, research has shown that we not only consciously prefer attractive people and that we associate their appearance with an inherent 'goodness' which then reflects directly on the product (also called the Halo effect), but that attractive faces instantly produce a positive feeling in the viewer. This instantaneous and unconscious (and therefore uncontrollable) 'goodness' association is produced irrespective of the gender of the viewer or the model. Interestingly, looking at attractive individuals produces similar physiological responses in viewers to those observed when people are presented with money. Thus, attractiveness works, and this signal

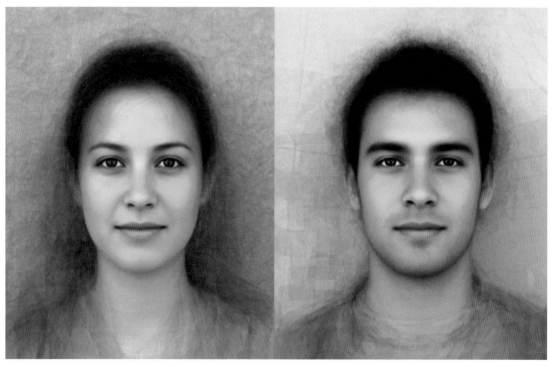

Surprisingly, an average face with average proportions
is not experienced as average, but as attractive. In fact,
averageness is to a large degree what attractiveness is.
The man and woman on the bottom are composites
(a "mean") of the individual faces seen above.

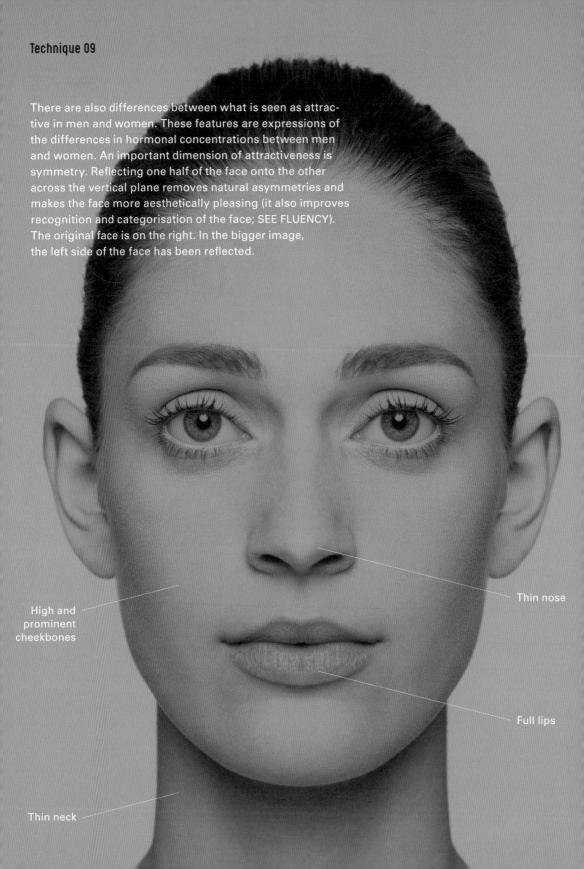

There are also differences between what is seen as attractive in men and women. These features are expressions of the differences in hormonal concentrations between men and women. An important dimension of attractiveness is symmetry. Reflecting one half of the face onto the other across the vertical plane removes natural asymmetries and makes the face more aesthetically pleasing (it also improves recognition and categorisation of the face; SEE FLUENCY). The original face is on the right. In the bigger image, the left side of the face has been reflected.

Thin nose

High and prominent cheekbones

Full lips

Thin neck

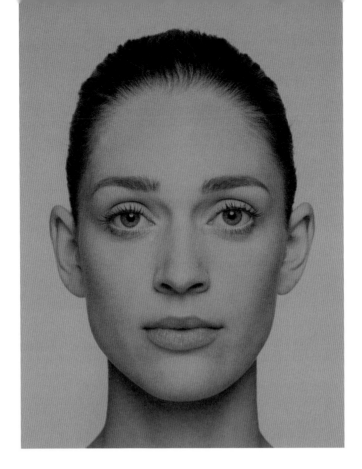

is pervasive, hard to ignore, and rewarding. Furthermore, few other persuasive techniques have the same ease-of-use-to-effectiveness ratio as a pretty face, as is clearly demonstrated by its widespread use – even for products completely unrelated to appearance.

Although bodily attractiveness is important, the face is often the first visual object one sees in human interactions and is generally considered the most important contribution to overall physical attractiveness. It is a common misconception that people with attractive faces seem arrogant, less intelligent, or even ditzy. These misconceptions are due to a misunderstanding about what facial attractiveness truly is. It is important to note that the attractiveness that has a fundamental positive effect when seen is that defined by biological markers; attractiveness is not defined by clothes, hairstyles, or make-up (although make-up can be used to enhance the qualities mentioned below). When we talk of facial attractiveness, we mean the fresh face you wake up with in the morning – your natural face.

Facial attractiveness is attributable to three main physical components:

1. **Averageness:** How prototypical or representative a face is.
2. **Symmetry:** The degree to which a face is symmetrical on the vertical axis.
3. **Sexual dimorphism:** The hormonal expression of sex-specific features, such as broad chins for men and high cheekbones for women.

An additional reason to consider incorporating (biologically determined) attractiveness in advertising is its universal application. Several surveys and experiments have shown a high personal consensus on facial attractiveness within and across cultures. Therefore, it has been suggested that facial beauty depends more on the inherent physical characteristics of the owner, rather than in the eyes of the perceiver. Even babies as young as six months show visual preferences for attractive faces. Therefore, when the faces used in advertisements are based on the right set of predictors, an attractive person will be perceived positively by all genders, ages, and cultures.

FINAL REMARKS → When one understands what is universally considered attractive, it can be implemented almost faultlessly in any campaign.

🔎 **Credibility, Face perception, Halo effect, Social modeling**

EFFECTIVENESS	X-FACTOR	IMPLEMENTATION
★ ★ ★ ★ ☆	★ ★ ★ ★ ☆	★ ★ ★ ★ ☆

HUMOUR

He who laughs is defenceless...

Humour is one of the most widely used techniques in advertising (about one third of all ads are intended to be humorous). However, until recently, scientists had a hard time understanding why brands and agencies used humour so often and how well it worked.

There are several types of humour, but the form used most often is incongruity-resolution. It involves an unusual, strange, or unexpected element in the ad (e.g., several people with white milk moustaches), which our brains try to make sense of (Got milk? Aha...it's a milk ad!). There are two steps: 1.) Thinking about the strange situation and trying to resolve it. 2.) Once resolved, we experience positive affect (find it funny) and may or may not laugh. Approximately 75% of humour used in ads is of this kind.

The use of humour in advertising is a fiercely debated topic. On the one hand some professionals distrust it and think that it is distracting and lures attention away from the core message the ad wants to convey. "People don't buy from clowns" sums up this camp. On the other hand, some professionals claim that it is always good to make people laugh and that it will make the brand well liked and "friendly."

Actually, both camps are right; humour is attention-grabbing and we will remember the joke well but the brand less well. However, on a more unconscious level, humour leads to positive feelings being associated

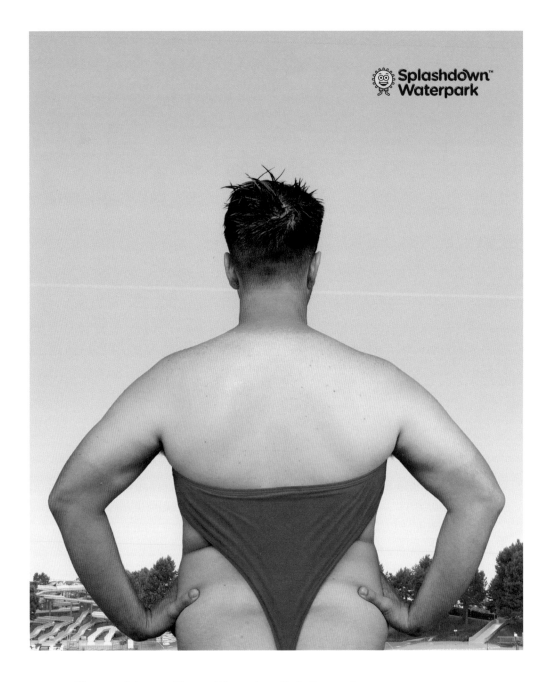

The surprising positions of the swimsuits in these ads attract viewers' attention. In combination with the brand (it's a water park!), the solution for the surprising situation is easily made: Splashdown's water slides are sooo fast, your swimsuit will end up in a funny location.

with the brand, even if we don't consciously remember the brand. Thesepositive feelings increase the chance that we will choose the brand associated with humour when shopping impulsively. Thus, it depends on an advertiser's goal as to whether humour is a good strategy to employ or not.

If the goal is to be "top-of-mind" when consumers are deliberately considering different brands for a product they'd like to buy, humour is not a good option. This is because although understanding humour increases remembering the joke, it decreases memory for the brand.

However, when the goal is to get people to buy a particular product while shopping, humour is actually a very good strategy to employ. This is especially true for situations in which customers need to make quick decisions or don't care too much, as their behaviour is mostly guided by

An example of subtle and intelligent humour, including an anthorpomorphistic element to the humour. At first glance, it's unclear what's going on. However, after reading the tagline "free your dog," it becomes clear to the viewer that the fat dog would rather be the active and fit dog he imagines himself to be.

intuition and affect. In these cases, when customers see a brand that was (unconsciously) paired with humour, they spontaneously choose it over brands not associated with humour.

An additional advantage to using humour is that it lowers resistance to advertising, and thus lowers the necessary marketing effort. When we laugh and pay attention to the joke, our moods are lifted and we pay less attention to being influenced (hence the starting quote of this technique). So if we are confronted with a marketing attempt (e.g., an ad, direct market- ing, or point-of-sale sales/actions) that comes from a humorous brand we feel less resistant towards it. Furthermore, on a societal level, humour is a great technique to use in ads because it decreases the annoyance we may experience from the daily bombardment of commercial messages we are confronted with. Humour in advertising is like every day social interactions: we prefer spending our time with someone who has a sense of humour and can make us laugh instead of with someone who is too serious.

FINAL REMARKS

→ Humour decreases memory for the brand, but increases liking of the brand.
→ Humour is especially beneficial when it comes to impulsive buying decisions.
→ Humour is good for the general acceptance of advertising.

🔎 **Duchennes Smiles, Humor and Dopamine, Disrupt and Reframe, Broaden-and-Build Theory**

EFFECTIVENESS | X-FACTOR | IMPLEMENTATION
★★★★☆ | ★★★★☆ | ★★★★☆

SCARCITY

If it is hard to get, people want it more

The most expensive things in life are scarce. It also works the other way around; when something seems scarce, it feels more valuable and we want to have it even more. In a classic 70s experiment, participants rated cookies from two different jars: one jar contained two cookies; the other 10 cookies. Although the cookies and the jars were identical, cookies from the jar containing fewer cookies (i.e., 2) were consistently rated as better tasting (cf. the jar containing 10 cookies).

The scarcity technique is based on influence attempts in which people are convinced to buy a product (or to do something) by believing that they need to act before the opportunity is gone. "Only one left," "Today only: 50% off," and "Three other potential buyers are interested in this house" are all examples of the scarcity technique in action. The technique's persuasive power comes down to perceived (un)availability; that is, the feeling that this is our last chance to obtain the offer, product, or opportunity. If we don't act now, we may pay more in the future or the product/deal might become unavailable – we'd regret it if we missed out!

The exact underlying psychological processes involved in persuasion by the scarcity technique are still debated, but several likely candidates play a role. First, people might hold a general heuristic, such as 'scarce objects are valuable.' This is an extension of the rule that most expensive things

LIMITED EDITION*

 SUPERHEROES MINIATURES SHOP   limitededition.c

LIMITED EDITION*

SUPERHEROES MINIATURES SHOP   limitededition.c

Many advertisements show their product front-on and add scarcity to their message, such as "Now or never," "Only X left," etc. This ad by Superheroes Miniatures Shop takes the use of scarcity a step further. The main message is 'limited edition' and only after a longer look will you discover that it concerns the limited edition of an action figure. The words 'limited edition' will attract attention. When something is limited, and you are lucky enough to see it in time, you could be one of the few proud owners of this exclusive item. The value in these products is that we feel they might be a real collector's item and worth a lot of money later. Note that limited edition ads almost never tell you how limited "limited" is. Unfortunately, they're probably not as limited as you'd like to imagine.

LAST CHANCE! ONLY 1 LEFT!

An area where scarcity is omnipresent is in online travel sales. Whether you want to buy a plane ticket, book a hotel room, or rent a car, after entering your location, arrival, and departure details, you'll receive your travel options surrounded by dark red letters stating: "Only 2 seats left!" or the more sophisticated "Girona airport seems busy at that time, the prices may go up soon." Knowing that the prices you see now may soon rise, that the hotel you see is almost full, or that the attractive car is about to be rented out will persuade you to decide quickly and to book immediately. Better to be safe than sorry!

BOOK NOW

in life really are scarce (e.g., gold and diamonds). Second, when an item is scarce (such as "Only 2 left"), this may be an indication that many other people also liked or already bought that product. When so many others want it, it must be good! (ALSO SEE SOCIAL PROOF, PAGE 48)

A third important explanation regarding scarcity is derived from reactance theory. When we have the option to buy a product or not, we have freedom. However, when something is scarce, we have that freedom now, but will lose it soon. That is, once the product is sold out, or otherwise unavailable, we lose our freedom to choose; we can only not buy the product. Thus, the idea is that when our freedom is threatened by messages employing scarcity, we buy the product in reaction to this threat.

Closely related to this is yet another ingredient: Anticipated regret. Anticipated regret is when we imagine how much regret we would feel if we made the "wrong" choice, and we take this into account when making decisions (SEE LOSS VS. GAIN FRAMING, PAGE 150). What if we later regret our decision to not buy that last pair of jeans? In this case, buying the jeans seems to be the best option because we can prevent feeling regret over an unavailable pair of jeans.

Obviously, the scarcity technique is easy to implement. Whether based on time ("Limited offer only"), quantity ("Only a few items left"), or competition ("Everyone is lining up, so make sure you get one"), advertisements often apply scarcity.

FINAL REMARKS

→ Scarce products are more attractive than non-scarce products.

→ People strive for a sense of freedom, and scarcity is a threat to people's freedom of choice.

→ When you are made to imagine how you would feel if you could not by a product, it makes you like the product more.

○ **Demand & Supply, Opportunity costs, Safety needs, Uncertainty avoidance**

EFFECTIVENESS	X-FACTOR	IMPLEMENTATION
★★★★☆	★★★★☆	★★★☆☆

FLEETING ATTRACTION

Feelings of similarity between a messenger and their target can double compliance

Have you ever given in to a request from a stranger to help, donate, or purchase a product, but later wondered why you gave in? Somehow you developed a positive feeling about this person; a sense of familiarity and liking. But, strangely, you can't put your finger on where these feelings came from or how they came about.

Not surprisingly, liking someone is the number one predictor for complying with another's request. We more readily help our good friends and those who are similar to us in terms of our opinions, values, or personalities. This is due to the so called "liking heuristic," coined by Shelly Chaiken, which states: "If I like you I'll go out of my way to please you." This is an obvious, but fundamental, human rule.

The liking of people whom we believe to be similar to us is so strong that even small, irrelevant experiences or signals of similarity unconsciously activate this mental shortcut. The researcher Jerry Burger has spent a long time showing the power of this so-called fleeting attraction, an induced form of temporary liking. In his experiments, he demonstrates that just having two people sit together in a room makes their future compliance rates with each other double. In other experiments, people filled out personality questionnaires and were subsequently shown the same questionnaires allegedly filled out by another person

(in reality they were filled out by the researchers). If participants believed
that they were similar to the other person, based on these fake tests,
they complied significantly more with this other person's requests later.
Now this may not sound very surprising, as (real) similarity is indeed
a good indicator of whether we should trust and help another person,
and the questionnaire indeed suggested that they were both similar on
important personality variables. However, the usefulness of this technique
in advertising becomes apparent when it is understood that even irrelevant
factors, like sharing a first name, has exactly the same effect. A name is
not indicative of any real similarity, but still increases liking and a positive
attitude towards the person. This effect occurs even when people are told
that they share a birth date.

Brands try to identify with their target group by playing on the target group's emotions and attitudes concerning life and society. These images and slogans suggest that "we are like you." In this way, the brand tries to convey that it is very close and similar to the target group, creating an in-group feeling.

A Coca Cola campaign introduced personalised cans and bottles by labelling them with popular male and female names, adapted to specific countries. People have automatic emotional reactions to and memories of the names of people they know and like. A consumer's own name may even happen to be on the bottle. These names create a sense of familiarity and similarity, which implicitly increases liking and a positive attitude towards the product.

However, it gets better! People who were told they have a special (but in reality, non-existent) fingerprint type complied much more with others whom they were told also had the same fingerprint. This shows that even fake similarities can be created to trigger fleeting attraction. The catch is that the similarity has to be felt as special; if it is a feature or characteristic we share with everyone (e.g., the person in the advertisement is a man and so are we) it will not work. The more distinctive the shared similarity is, the more impact it will have.

A few factors that create fleeting attraction through perceived similarity are: spending time together (SEE MERE EXPOSURE, PAGE 90), same names, same birth dates, similar clothing, same academic titles, similar geographic backgrounds, same music preferences; and same religious affiliations or backgrounds.

This technique is, therefore, especially relevant for the growing market of individually targeted advertisements. Ads on the internet can tap into personal information and use this to provide fake signals of similarity and thereby a sense of fleeting attraction. Next generation advertising, where salespeople wear Google glasses, could easily employ this strategy by summoning personal information from social networking sites before or while serving a customer. If you are greeted by someone who shares your name or interests, this will create an effective starting position for negotiations.

FINAL REMARKS
→ Similarities need to be presented before the target present theirs. If presented afterwards, as in: "Oh your name is Lisa, so is mine," it can be detected as a ruse.
→ Inducing fleeting attraction through similarity has proven most effective on people with high needs for social approval and affiliation.

🔎 **Bonding, Interpersonal attraction, Rapport**

EFFECTIVENESS	X-FACTOR	IMPLEMENTATION
★★★★☆	★★★★☆	★★☆☆☆

DECOY

When consumers are choosing between two similar products, introducing a decoy can push people towards the desired direction

The decoy is designed so that one of two original options becomes asymmetrically dominant to the decoy option. So, in a hypothetical situation, while options A and B are seemingly equal, only one of these (e.g., A) is obviously better than an added option, the decoy, C. The goal of adding the decoy, C, is not to have people chose C, but to give A the appearance of higher value and to make people chose this over B. Think about this: How can it be that an equally existing preference for A or B can be changed to either A's or B's advantage just by adding a third option, C? No matter how good (or bad) C is, the differences or similarities between A and B are objectively unchanged. Truly, this technique is just more proof that man is not a rational agent and/or a logical consumer. Our brain is our own worst enemy and advertisers know it!

Let's further demonstrate this abstract technique by providing an example. Say you want to purchase the new black IPhone X. Your options are the following: A) €799 for 64GB; or B) €999 for 256GB. This could be a difficult choice. Some will prefer A for the price; others B for the storage capacity. But what if we now add an extra option, C – the decoy. It is about as expensive as B, but has less storage. Option C: €959, 128GB. Now, suddenly, B seems like a better deal because you don't pay much more than you would for C, but get a lot more space. More people choose B over A than

before the decoy was added and nobody in their right mind chooses C.
To reiterate, B (rather than A) is now asymmetrically dominant to C.

Neuroimaging techniques have been used to explore this odd and illog-ical bias. Such studies have found that when it is difficult for us to choose between two equally preferred options, adding a decoy reduces our stress reactions by lowering the feeling of conflicting information. This is because the decoy provides additional information, which helps to "unveil" the superior option, thereby easing the decision-making process.

Interestingly, no matter how well-informed people are about this tech-nique and how explicitly it is applied, it is almost undetectable. Anything can be advertised using the decoy effect: from beers and snacks, to televi-sions, cars, and even politicians (e.g., just add a third, decoy, politician who is asymmetrically inferior to only one of the candidates).

FINAL REMARKS

→ The decoy must always be presented subtly as the least-favoured option.

→ The decoy technique works best for high-quality (cf. low-quality) products.

○ **Agenda-setting, Distinction bias, Phantom options, Proposal-reframing**

S

€2,-

M

€4,-

The use of decoys can often be found in the food and beverage service industry. Imagine you are in a café and you want a coffee. The small cup costs €2, the medium one €4, and the large coffee costs €5. Here, the medium coffee is the decoy. You may not even want a large coffee, but it sure seems like a good deal compared to the medium one.

| EFFECTIVENESS | X-FACTOR | IMPLEMENTATION |
| ★ ★ ★ ★ ☆ | ★ ★ ★ ☆ ☆ | ★ ★ ★ ☆ ☆ |

THAT'S NOT ALL

Spontaneously offering a discount or offering free extras before the sales pitch is even over

"This amazing knife set sells for only €69.95, BUT that's not all! For no extra cost we will add this titanium cutting board and another knife set." Teleshopping used to be a popular television format in the pre-digital era, toting home trainers, beauty creams, knives, and pot and pan sets. You name it, they sold it. It was one of the first advertising platforms delving deeply into social influence and persuasion techniques. The most infamous of these techniques is probably the 'that's not all' (TNA) technique. After presenting the product and its price, the product pitcher would enter a final phase of adding extra items or bonuses without changing the original price. The initial deal already sounded good, but now sounds amazing!

The main psychological process that makes this technique work is feeling the need to respond to the negotiations by the seller (SEE RECIPROCITY, PAGE 130). The addition of extras or discounts gives the impression that the seller is making a concession. Second, the key is to have people believe that the initial deal was supposed to sell for that sum. Then everything extra would indeed be "free".

It is already clear to you that the TNA technique is strikingly simple. An initial request is followed by something that sweetens the deal further (a discount, a gift, a gadget, or an incentive) before the target can even

€ 89,95
NOW
€69,95

The knife set mentioned in the intro of this chapter.
The first knife's original price is displayed as €89,95.
But wait! We'll give you a discount! Now it's only
€69,95. Not good enough? Well there's more!
We'll throw in another knife for free, and another
one, and so on. In the end it sounds too good to be
true: Buyers get ALL of these products for the price
of just ONE discounted knife.

You're interested in buying this magazine?
But wait, that's not all! There are three
more gifts you will receive for free.
Of course these items are, by definition,
not free because you have to buy the
magazine in order to get them. Note:
The "No.1" button on the top left is
also representing a kind of authority.

think or react to the first offer. Importantly, presenting the little extra(s) in quick succession has a stronger effect than when the products are presented simultaneously at the start. One of the original TNA experiments demonstrated that it was much easier to sell a muffin and two cookies for 75 cents when the muffin was advertised for 75 cents first and then the cookies were thrown into the deal than when selling them together for 75 cents. Furthermore, a muffin sold more easily when the initial price was $1, but was lowered immediately to 75 cents than when the muffin was already advertised at 75 cents.

The TNA technique works better for low-cost items (i.e., where targets are less cognitively involved to evaluate the product and its estimated worth). A more expensive product or a product that one is specifically looking for stimulates a more mindful consideration of the product – its quality and costs – and would gain little benefit from using the TNA. But that's not all! Free TNA implementation tips under final remarks!

FINAL REMARKS
→ The initial offer needs to appear reasonable.
→ The discount or extra(s) has to follow the initial offer in stages.
→ A recipient should not have an opportunity to respond to each extra offer. Offering is continued until the presentation is finished.
→ For maximum effect, the final "bonus" should be particularly desirable.

🔍 **'It's free!' bias, Reciprocity**

15

MERE EXPOSURE

The more we see it, the more we like it

While it seems intuitive that repeated exposure keeps stimulating your desire for a product or brand and helps to commit brands to memory, this is not the only reason big brands keep pushing themselves into your visual surroundings. Research shows that material which is neutral or positive in nature is experienced as more positive upon repeated presentation. This effect is due to an increased feeling of familiarity, and it holds for all visual stimuli people encounter – people and products alike. The more often you see that new person in the office and the more often you pass by that new soft drink poster, the more positive you feel about them.

In 1968, a researcher named Robert Zajonc cleverly demonstrated the existence of this unconscious effect when he showed that people preferred meaningless Chinese symbols when they had been shown repeatedly compared to when they had only been seen once. This demonstrated that material empty of emotional or meaningful content could become positively laden simply by the means of presentation. Advertisement companies know that just through flooded exposure to a product or a brand people start liking it more, without ever having reflected upon why. When asked, people might not even recognise the product, while still reporting warm feelings towards it. This unconscious positive affect translates into buying behaviour, especially when people's personal preference for competing brands is low

For most of us, this is an unfamiliar Chinese character. However, if you were to look at this page every day from now on, you'd develop more positive feelings about it. As described in the text, Robert Zajonc performed a world-famous experiment (in 1968), where he showed Chinese characters to American, non-Chinese speaking participants from one to 25 times, and asked them to guess their meaning. The more times participants had seen a character previously, the more positive their predictions were about the meaning of the character. By the way, this Chinese character means 'repetition.'

Billions of dollars are spent by big consumer brands to maximise their exposure. As explained in the text, such exposure not only makes us remember and consider the brand when we are about to buy a product, but also makes us feel good about the brand. The mere exposure effect can produce some interesting results, however. For example, in retail questionnaires, people often indicate that they look for unique and "hidden" boutiques when shopping; however, when they actually go shopping, they end up in the same old big clothing chains. When we travel from Amsterdam to Shanghai and go to a mall, there's a big chance we'll just walk into the next H&M.

and/or when engaging in impulse shopping. A perfect example is Coca Cola. Their brand name and slogan is unavoidable – television ads and billboards are omnipresent. Constant re-presentation of the brand has resulted in worldwide familiarity, which creates positive associations by mere exposure. Of course people can be overexposed to stimuli, creating effects opposite to what is desired. Experiments show that the mere exposure technique reaches its maximum effect within ten to twenty presentations.

Another less intrusive, but equally effective, form of mere exposure is product placements in films, TV series, music videos, etc. Since no attention is overtly directed at the product, it does not feel like an advertisement, which keeps reactance to the influence attempt low. Additionally, these products can be connected to popular actors or characters for an (often unconscious) positivity boost.

In sum, the mere exposure technique is easy to apply (provided one has the budget for repeated marketing), and mostly affects unconscious buying behaviour and impulsive decision-making. If you want others to like you more, you'd better make sure they see you around!

FINAL REMARKS

→ The first ten to twenty exposures are the most important; after this, each added exposure has a somewhat reduced impact on increased liking (but of course, it keeps the item in mind).

→ Exposures should be kept brief, with sufficient delays between presentations to avoid overexposure effects.

🔎 **Availability heuristic, Familiarity effect, Propinquity effect**

16

EFFECTIVENESS | X-FACTOR | IMPLEMENTATION
★★★★☆ | ★★☆☆☆ | ★★★☆☆

ANCHORING

A product's value is strongly influenced by what it is compared to

Anchoring is a complex cognitive bias, whereby we use existing information as a baseline for our new judgements and decisions. The easiest way to explain the anchoring technique is by demonstration. Answer the following questions in sequence before reading on:

Is the Nile shorter or longer than 200 miles?
What is your estimation of its length?

The estimations people give to this second question become wildly different when the number in the first question is replaced with 10,000 (miles). The number included in the first question becomes a comparison anchor from which one departs when estimating the real length. In response to the first case, people are more likely to report the Nile's length as 300 miles, while in the second case estimates average 7,000 miles. New judgements are always compared internally to existing information and are then adjusted towards or away from this standard. The extent to which false illusory anchors can be used to influence our judgements depends on our prior knowledge of the topic: The less we know, the more we rely on new information as an anchor. The Nile is, in fact, 4,130 miles long.

When compared to dressing up a dog for 11 minutes,
or texting "important" messages for 26 minutes, brushing your
teeth twice a day for two minutes isn't a significant challenge.

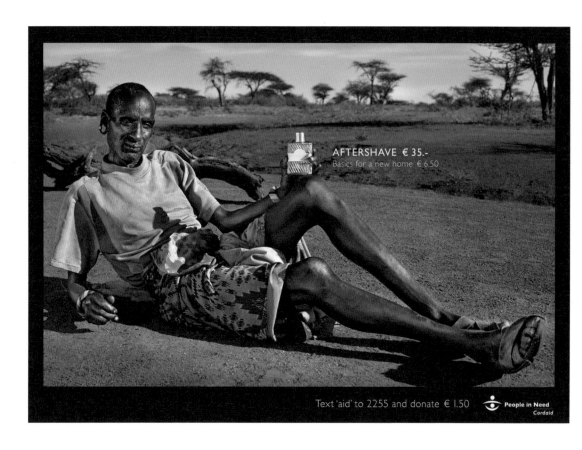

AFTERSHAVE € 35.-
Basics for a new home € 6.50

Text 'aid' to 2255 and donate € 1.50   People in Need
Cordaid

Here is another classic example by Tversky and Kahneman,
the discoverers of this bias:

What is the sum of the following multiplication:
1 x 2 x 3 x 4 x 5 x 6 x 7 x 8?
OR, what is the sum of the following:
8 x 7 x 6 x 5 x 4 x 3 x 2 x 1?

Interestingly, when the first number (the anchor) is 1, people's mean
estimate is 512; however, when the first number is 8, the mean estimate
dramatically increases to 2,250. The answer, for both, is 40,320.
The first number then (small or large) sets our expectation for the size
of the multiplication.

HANDBAG € 32.-
Food for a week € 4.-

Text 'aid' to 2255 and donate € 1,50   People in Need
Cordaid

Cordaid's request is to donate €1.50 to help African communities improve their basic living environment. They compare prices of luxurious products we normally buy for ourselves (e.g., €35 for aftershave) with what a home costs in some African communities (€ 6.50). By setting these standards, the required donation (€1.50) seems very small.

Anchoring may also explain why people spend more money right after pay day – a high balance gives the impression of surplus wealth. Even when we consciously know that the future will be less rose-coloured, this balance sets the anchor for our spending behaviour.

The implications of anchoring for marketing are obvious. If we believe that a car is worth €3,000 and it's purchased for €1,500 we believe we are getting a great deal; however, this is not so if we believe that the original worth is €1,600. Thus, in marketing, original prices or standards are consciously set with the negotiation goal in mind. Obviously, it is extremely easy to provide an effective fake anchor when we, the buyers, are not automobile experts. Thus, a car salesman always starts with too high a price. Any setting where people use a numerical norm has the potential for the use of anchoring.

This bias has been shown to be almost impossible to overcome: Even when people are told that they are susceptible to anchoring and that it will be included in the information they are about to receive, they still do not correct for it sufficiently. Even experts (like judges, doctors, and seasoned consumers) fall for it! In sum, researchers have described the anchoring effect as easy to produce, but hard to explain (although we did our best!).

FINAL REMARKS

→ People in a good mood are less analytical, and therefore are more sensitive to anchoring.

→ Start low when bidding. This sets the baseline, and others will adapt their counteroffers accordingly. The technique even works when the initial bid is obviously too low.

→ Non-specific anchors (e.g., €100) work better for negotiating larger price adjustments than specific ones (e.g., €99.99), as they indicate the increments by which future adjustments will increase or decrease (dollars or cents, respectively).

🔎 **Adjustment heuristic , Focalism**

EFFECTIVENESS | X-FACTOR | IMPLEMENTATION
★★★★☆ | ★★☆☆☆ | ★★☆☆☆

ASTROTURFING

Fake social proof is used
to create an impression of popular support

Astroturf originally refers to the artificial grass that is often found on sports fields. Here astroturfing means creating an illusion that people similar to you (the grassroots) support a specific idea or product. The practice is much wider spread than believed and is a sure sign that companies understand just how often we look to others to guide our own opinions and behaviours. Especially in the online world, this method is often used to influence decision-making.

Some experts have estimated that one third of all consumer reviews are fake – for example, sponsored by invested parties. The recent development of advanced "persona management" software (which creates fake but believable aliases, profiles, and locations) makes it increasingly hard to detect who someone in the cybersphere really is. Some ingenious companies now offer positive book reviews on Amazon and other online markets. Digital Facebook 'likes' and Twitter 'followers' can literally be bought by the thousands to increase the apparent number of supporters, thereby creating an illusion of importance, trust, and social proof.

Other examples include: independent individuals who are paid to criticise or remove negative comments on online fora and platforms (e.g., delete or change information on Wikipedia); blogs containing glowing product reviews, which appear to be written by independent consumers, but are actually sponsored by the producers; and patient support groups or doctors who recommend specific products, but are sponsored by pharmaceutical companies.

For the individual consumer, it is very difficult to discover forms of online astroturfing. However, if the consumer does manage to detect and reveal the use of astroturfing, it will likely result in a boomerang effect; that is, with the customer developing a negative attitude towards the company or brand as a consequence. Such discoveries are spread quickly and easily throughout the World Wide Web and can have long-lasting negative effects for the company in question.

FINAL REMARKS   → Astroturfing is unethical, dishonest, and unfair.
It should be avoided when companies want to be seen
as trustworthy, believable and authentic.

🔍 **Agenda-setting, False flag operations,
Internet water army, Viral marketing**

Want more exposure?
We send real people to like your Page!

$69
1000
👍 Likes
Try it Now!

$198
5000
👍 Likes
Try it Now!

$298
10000
👍 Likes
Try it Now!

Buy facebook likes! More 'likes' show more social support and trust. In the digital world the question this raises is how 'real' are all these likes, Twitter followers or product reviews?

"

The secret of
my influence
has always
been that
it remained
secret.

SALVADOR DALÍ
surrealist

18

EFFECTIVENESS | X-FACTOR | IMPLEMENTATION
★★★☆☆ | ★★★★★ | ★★★★☆

ANTHROPOMORPHISM

When a brand or product is seen as human-like,
people will like it more and feel closer to it

Anthropomorphism is the tendency to describe and visualise animals
or non-living things using human characteristics. For example, "This car
is a spicy little race monster; she loves it when you step on the gas."

Throughout the history of mankind, humans have been prone to
explaining various events – such as the forces of nature or the behaviour
of animals – by ascribing intentionality, thoughts, or needs to those events
as if they were human. For example, "Nature (or even Mother Earth) is
angry and brewing up a storm" or "This chicken is unhappy in her cage
and wants to be out in the forest where she will feel free."

Anthropomorphism is also present during our early development;
as children we can become attached to a piece of cloth, play with stuffed
animals, or cry when watching Bambi (the Disney movie). Even when we
become older and wiser, our brain continues to try to see the things around
us as human-like (note: This sentence itself is an example of anthropomorphism). Although Pinocchio (in the Disney movie) is nothing more than an
animation of a wooden puppet, when we watch it with our children we will
cheer for the little puppet, cry with him, share his dreams and emotions,
and experience warm-and-fuzzy feelings at the movie's happy ending.

The great ape and the polar bear express emotions resembling human shame or disbelief. Secondary emotions (such as shame, disbelief, guilt, pride, etc.) are thought to be unique to humans, whereas primary emotions (such as fear, anger, happiness, etc.) are thought to be shared with other species. The expressed emotions thus suggest human-like features, resulting in influence via two means: we feel closer to the animals and share their shame and disbelief. Consequently, we are stimulated to donate to WWF.

Refisal adds potentially beneficial additives to its salt products. These ingredients, such as folic acid and iron, are related to fitness, strength, and health. In this ad, Refisal demonstrates what a healthy additive does: it improves the health of the food you eat. In this case, the salt with additives makes the chicken or broccoli more beneficial for the consumer. The anthropomorphism is expressed by the coach-athlete metaphor, making the role of the product in relation to food easy to understand and "feel" more attractive.

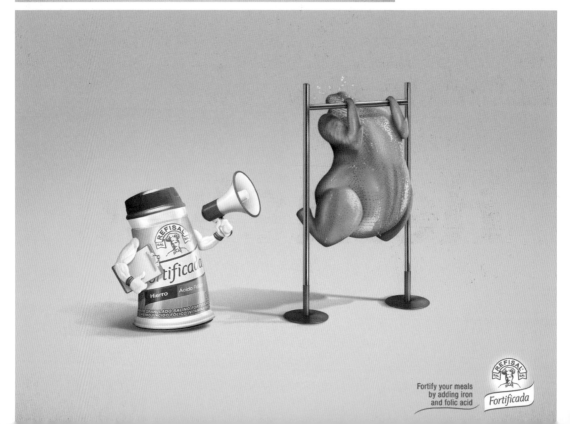

Biopark projects the human attributes "clean" versus "junkie" onto vegetables. No pesticides, additives, etc. means healthier vegetables! Who wants to expose themselves or their family to "junkie" vegetables?

Heineken

The famous Heineken example: By tilting the e's in Heineken backwards slightly, they seem to smile. This makes the logo appear more happy and friendly, and thus more human-like.

Anthropomorphism makes us bond with objects. When we anthropomorphise, we think that the object, brand, product, or animal is actually more like us. We tend to add thoughts and emotions to objects in a similar way to how we would experience things ourselves, which stimulates liking and empathy for the object. The more we like an advertised product and have "feelings" for it, the more likely we are to bond with it, and thus buy the advertised product.

Although our brain loves to anthropomorphise and will try to do it whenever possible (there we go again!), techniques can be used in advertising to enhance this effect. In visual ads, we can give an object the human form, such as a human shape, limbs, a face, facial expressions, etc. Alternatively, in text, we can describe an object in a human-like way by providing feelings, thoughts it may have, or an experience it may undergo. In television commercials, objects can be humanised just by letting them move and behave purposefully or by making the objects sound like humans.

Of course, when making a product human-like, it should be sympathetic; otherwise a strong dislike for the product or disidentification with the object may be induced.

FINAL REMARKS

→ People want to bond with brands and products, so try to make establishing the bond as easy as possible.
→ Use human-like shapes and behaviours to increase anthropomorphism.
→ When humans anthropomorphise, they will not only see a product as more human-like (in general), but also as more like themselves.

🔎 **Empathy, Personification, Similarity, Simulation**

THE LIFE OF A PLANT
IS HARDER THAN IT SEEMS.

Vigor Plant sells materials to hobbyists and professionals to improve the health of plants. Selling such products is easier when people have the idea that plants need them. Instead of describing how beautiful they will look, Vigor Plant suggests that plants may suffer (and how you can solve that by buying Vigor Plant), using the crown of thorns symbol famous from Jesus's suffering. This makes the plant more human-like (or Jesus-like) and increases our urge to help the "poor" plant.

Happy plants.

EFFECTIVENESS	X-FACTOR	IMPLEMENTATION
★★★☆☆	★★★★☆	★★★★☆

TRUSTWORTHINESS

A trustworthy face is worth a thousand words

People rely on informative cues, such as medals, diplomas, awards, and letters of recommendation (SEE AUTHORITY, PAGE 145) to discern whether a source is credible. Uniforms and other clothing cues are another way to quickly signal to others that a message comes from a reliable source. Consequently, including these cues in advertisements gives the impression of trustworthiness.

However, the most striking detection of trustworthiness occurs in facial perception. We automatically process all sorts of facial features and make (un)conscious inferences from those features. This occurs with a great consensus, suggesting that universal physical cues are used to quickly judge people on certain traits (e.g., aggressiveness and extraversion). The information extracted most quickly from a face is trustworthiness (even quicker than attractiveness). The facial width-to-height ratio (fWHR) is the cue most often linked to judgements of trustworthiness. The fWHR is the ratio between the width (the distance between the two extremes of the cheekbones) and the height (the distance between the upper lip to the eyebrow) of the face. When faces are relatively high (cf. wide) they are perceived as more trustworthy compared to relatively wide faces.

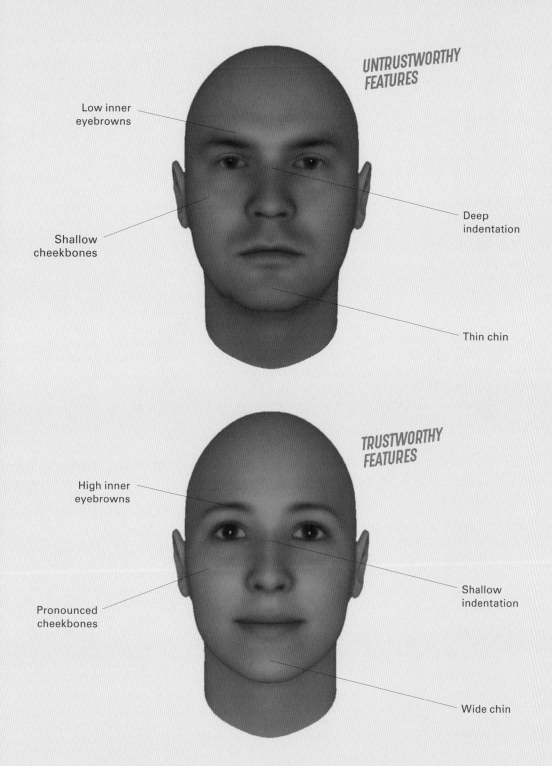

UNTRUSTWORTHY FEATURES

Low inner eyebrowns

Shallow cheekbones

Deep indentation

Thin chin

TRUSTWORTHY FEATURES

High inner eyebrowns

Pronounced cheekbones

Shallow indentation

Wide chin

Least trustworthy   Neutral   Most trustworthy

The 2 figures in this chapter give an overview of several indices (complementary to the fWHR) our brains use unconsciously to make inferences about the trustworthiness of the people we see. Based on these indices, we, the 3 authors of this book, may be lucky that it is a book and not a DVD. Of course the smile is important too. To quote Mother Teresa, a great ambassador for the power of a smile: "Peace begins with a smile." But note that a slow onset of a smile is seen as more trustworthy than one with a fast onset.

Related to this, brown eyes are rated as more trustworthy than blue eyes, most likely because eye colour is correlated with facial features perceived unconsciously as either happy (brown) or angry (blue). Examples of other facial features signaling trustworthiness are eye size, smile type, and babyfaceness.

There is a strong debate about whether the fWHR, or similar facial features, are actually related to trustworthy behaviour. Is someone with a high fWHR really less trustworthy than someone with a low fWHR? At best, there may be a small relation; however, many studies have found no relation at all, meaning it could purely be in the eyes of the beholder.

Of course, even though these facial features do not appear to make substantial predictions about behaviour, as long as humans have the strong and universal tendency to unconsciously and spontaneously relate them to trustworthiness it is a good idea to keep them in mind when selecting models for a campaign or an ad.

In addition, trustworthiness is fairly easily altered graphically using photo manipulation software. This means that real and virtual models or agents can be made to look maximally trustworthy.

FINAL REMARKS

→ We judge faces spontaneously on trustworthiness and we will feel more positive towards ads containing trustworthy faces.

→ Our judgements of trustworthiness don't predict how much you can really trust a person, but we still let this judgement inform our decisions.

→ Other non-physical cues of trustworthiness (e.g., medals, recommendations, job titles etc.) also affect our feelings towards an ad or product.

🔎 **Credibility, Expertise-oxcytocin (hormone), Facial asymmetry**

EFFECTIVENESS | X-FACTOR | IMPLEMENTATION
★★★☆☆ | ★★★★☆ | ★★★☆☆

DISRUPT & REFRAME

Disrupting attention gives advertisers an opportunity to reframe and resell an already dismissed proposal

Sometimes it is necessary to get a person out of their stable mindset in order to make them open to new information. When people are uninterested, fixed in their normal routine, resistant, or just not attending to you, you can use a crowbar technique, such as disruption. When targets are disrupted or surprised, their attention is captured and they are then more likely to comply with a subsequent proposal.

Disruption techniques introduce an unexpected element, which attracts the attention of the audience and momentarily disables their critical thinking. This then "opens the gate" to further persuasion and compliance. For example, instead of asking for "money," a panhandler could ask for "39 cents." This unusual request is the disruption; it attracts attention, disables initial resistance, and instantly leads to more "Yes" responses.

The disrupt-then-reframe technique (DTR) also uses the element of surprise, but then continues with a reframing of the proposal. For example, a salesperson may say, "This deck of cards costs 300 cents (disrupt)... That's 3 dollars. It's a bargain (reframe)!" First, the surprise is used to get people out of their usual resistance against salespeople. Subsequently, their attention and cognitive processes will be applied to interpreting the unusual event. The reframing element helps the target to interpret the situation in a positive manner (oh, 300 cents is just 3 dollars!).

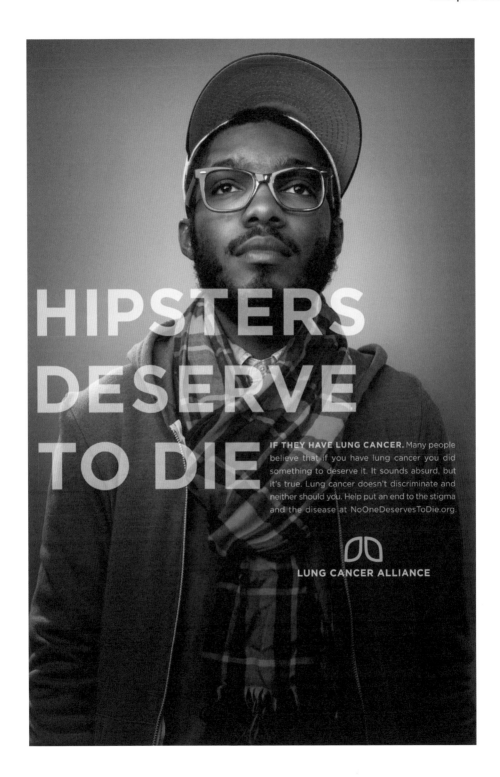

HIPSTERS DESERVE TO DIE

IF THEY HAVE LUNG CANCER. Many people believe that if you have lung cancer you did something to deserve it. It sounds absurd, but it's true. Lung cancer doesn't discriminate and neither should you. Help put an end to the stigma and the disease at NoOneDeservesToDie.org.

LUNG CANCER ALLIANCE

The counterintuitive message that "hipsters," "cat lovers," or "the tattooed" deserve to die makes you stop and try to make sense of what's going on. The reframe in the text to the right of the ads explains that it concerns lung cancer, and that often people think that patients with lung cancer did something to deserve it (e.g., smoking) or that they have "bad genes." This ad attempts to persuade the viewers that it can happen to anyone, and thus everybody should get involved and donate money to stop this disease.

Thus, disruption techniques either focus on grabbing the target's attention or on changing their perception of the situation. These techniques are widely used and very easy to apply in visual communications. For instance, images can also draw on this technique by showing surprising, strange, and unexpected features. In addition, the surprising element is often funny (a key ingredient in humour is an unexpected element or inconsistency; SEE HUMOUR, PAGE 67). However, while disruptions are closely linked to humour, they don't necessarily need to be funny to be effective; just unusual.

The boundaries of effectiveness with these techniques are reached when things get too weird or the situation is perceived negatively by the audience. The unexpected element should not scare or disgust people; that would likely lead to an avoidance of the ad, rather than directing attention towards it. In addition, the message involved needs to be conducive to getting a positive response. That is, just inducing a surprise without a clear message or request will not work. Finally, the initial surprise has to be followed by either a new interpretation or the possibility to act.

FINAL REMARKS

→ DTR originated in door-to-door sales situations. A potential customer is overwhelmed by irrelevant information from a fast-talking salesman and thereby becomes more susceptible to suggestion.

→ DTR is also often used during on-stage hypnosis. It makes people lose their guard for a moment, so that they no longer resist entering a trance state.

🔎 **Emotional seesaw, Foot-in-mouth, Pique technique**

I love to be single is looking for partner.

For all life's twists and turns:
Flexible financial plans.

The text in the ad clearly represents the disruption technique by being either grammatically incorrect or just plain incomprehensible. The reframe is in the smaller text, explaining that it represents changes occurring throughout our lives. For example, first you were single (and loving it), but now you are in a relationship. Or first you prioritised your career, but now you have children and they form your primary interest. SwissLife plays on the disrupt technique by showing that new and disrupting situations or perspectives may require new financial plans.

My career is the most important thing are my children.

For all life's twists and turns:
Flexible financial plans.

SwissLife

ONE CHILD IS HOLDING SOMETHING
THAT'S BEEN BANNED IN AMERICA
TO PROTECT THEM.
GUESS WHICH ONE.

We keep 'Little Red Riding Hood' out of schools because of the bottle of wine in her basket. Why not assault weapons?
MOMSDEMANDACTION.ORG

MOMS DEMAND ACTION
FOR GUN SENSE IN AMERICA

A provocative and attention grabbing image in light of school shootings, such as Columbine. The image of an armed pupil next to a classmate holding an innocuous object surprises and immediately motivates the viewer to search for its meaning. The accompanying headline alludes to an unexpected answer and encourages people to reappraise the image to resolve the puzzle. The quick and demanding cognitive shift necessary to identify this image's meaning temporarily lowers resistance to the message. A word of caution, however: Extremely provocative imagery may result in rebound effects.

| EFFECTIVENESS | X-FACTOR | IMPLEMENTATION |
| ★★★☆☆ | ★★★★☆ | ★★★☆☆ |

METAPHORS

The pen is mightier than the sword

A good metaphor can move people more than even the best arguments can. Supporting that people instinctively know this, some estimates claim that English speakers utter about one metaphor per 25 words! The use of metaphors generates feelings and ideas purely by associations, which are exceedingly hard to counter-argue with logic.

In short, metaphors simplify and play on the emotional and mnemonic shortcuts we use to guide behaviour. If the competition is "tough," we must arm ourselves and take them out first with force. If the economy is "dying" we must quickly develop a medicine or antidote for the disease that has stricken it. If an operating system is a "mountain lion" it must be strong, adaptive, efficient, and exotic.

What a metaphor does, then, is to propose that two unrelated objects or domains share important properties. Which properties they are is only limited by creativity – what a product or an idea can be compared to has no logical boundary. The metaphor only needs to target the audience's imagination and emotions. When hearing, reading, or seeing, a metaphor, we experience the original concept or product as being similar to the metaphor. This experience is important, as we would not understand the metaphor without it. The moment we understand a metaphoric compari-son, an association is unavoidably created, and because it is only a mental association, we cannot use our rationality to argue against it.

A metaphor proposes that two unrelated objects or domains share important properties. The relationship of two elements can be based on a connection ('A is associated with B'), a similarity ('A is like B'), or an opposition ('A is not like B'). Sometimes we need a little time to understand the metaphor, but once understood the association is unavoidably created. There are three main structures for a visual metaphor: juxtaposition (two side-by-side images), fusion (two combined images), and replacement (the present image points to an absent image). This Sekai ad shows a large, strong lion in the centre of the ad, ready to be taken for a walk. The car is presented in the left corner of the ad. Using a juxtaposition approach, these images create a connection, such that the attributes of the lion are associated with the car.

TRITON SAVANA

BYE
CHANGE YOUR HEAD

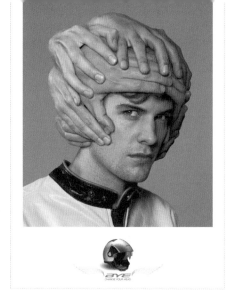

The Esso brand never meant we should put a real tiger in our tank. However, concepts of strength, power, and prowess are inevitably activated by this gas-tiger association. The beauty of associations is that it is the perceiver who unconsciously creates these sub-associations. For this reason, it is exceptionally easy to compare any product, offer, or service to a concept that is universally understood as being extraordinarily positive (e.g., as powerful as two suns, larger than life, etc.) and to get away with it – no matter how ridiculous the comparison is!

Because of the indirect language and visuals used in metaphors, it takes longer for us to detect false metaphors than when such a claim is literal. This is due, in part, to a concept known as syntactic indeterminacy. Since literal language always follows a logical structure and makes clear claims, these can be easily dissected and tested. The syntax of an image or metaphor, however, is more veiled and is not designed to describe reality; it is therefore indeterminate. We cannot easily counter-argue associations and stories that are mere suggestions.

The Bye helmets advertisement shows a metaphor using replacement. The helmet is replaced by hands, layered over each other in the shape of a helmet, protecting the sensitive head in a careful and secure way. This imagery establishes a feeling of trust and comfort.

Technique 21

In this campaign, the metaphorical dimension of the image gives the answer to the rhetorical question posed in the right upper corner, "Where does your rubbish go?" By throwing your rubbish on the ground it will ultimately end up in the water. The metaphor is established by fusing two images: the ground and the representation of the physicality of water.

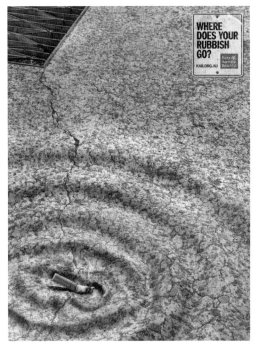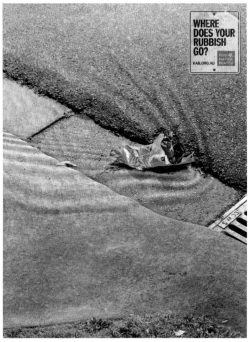

FINAL REMARKS

→ When describing something positive, lively and active metaphors are best (e.g., "The value of your house is climbing"), but when something negative is described, it is better to use dead and inactive metaphors (e.g., "The value of your house fell"). These guidelines highlight the purposefulness and action-readiness of the positive situation, while making the negative one feel less threatening.

→ Metaphors should be positioned at the start of a sentence or proposition. It then becomes the lens through which subsequent information is interpreted.

→ The current fashion is to use 'green', organic or biological metaphors to describe products. Computers, cars, and pens then radiate some of the majestic power of nature.

🔍 **Allegory, Hyperbole, Labeling, Simile**

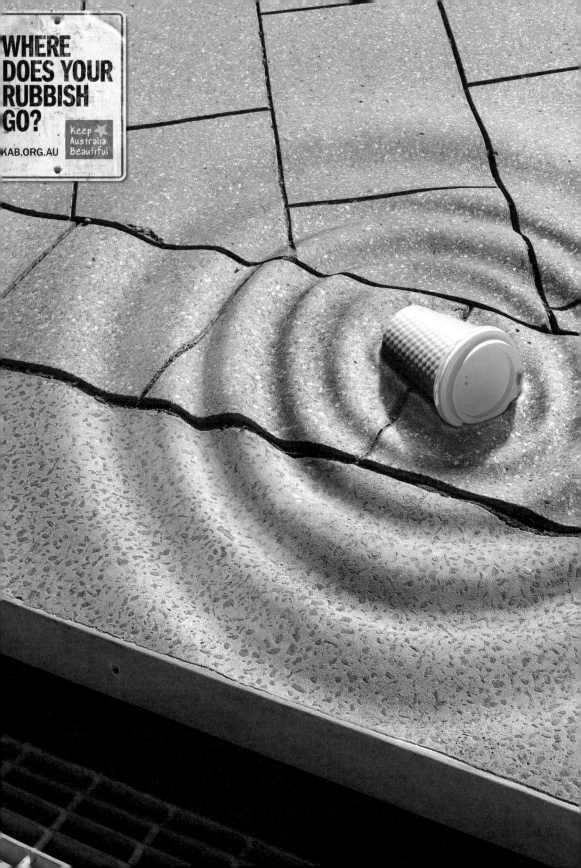

22

EFFECTIVENESS | X-FACTOR | IMPLEMENTATION
★★★ ★ ★ | ★★★★ ★ | ★★ ★ ★ ★

IMPLEMENTATION INTENTIONS

Implementation intentions help people to reach their goals step by step

When people hold a positive attitude towards engaging in a particular behaviour, it doesn't necessarily mean they will act on it. For instance, when you have an abstract goal, such as "I would like to lose weight, "you can live your life having that goal, but never actually put it into action. Procrastination or a lack of urgency may result in you repeatedly thinking "I'll start tomorrow." Implementation intentions, however, require you to make a plan (intention) about how you will perform (implement) a certain behaviour or goal. With an implementation intention, you make a concrete plan about where and when you will achieve your goal, for example: "Today at 5 pm, after work, I will go to the gym." In that case, you'll either succeed or fail – there is no ambiguity about whether or not the goal has been met.

In addition, by planning the action concretely, the set time (i.e., 5 pm) will serve as a cue to act. That is, when the clock strikes 5 pm, this visual cue may remind you of your plan to go to the gym. Implementations have been shown to work across a variety of behaviours, and lasting effects have been obtained. Although especially employed in the areas of health and environmental behaviours, this technique can be applied to almost any behaviour where there is a risk that a plan will not be executed. However, behaviours that are rewarding in themselves, such as drinking beer, mating, and eating fast-food do not need this "helping hand."

SWITCH OFF
UNPLUG
SAVE!
I PLEDGE TO SAVE 10%

The eThekwini municipality in South Africa (around Durban) attempts to make people perform specific energy saving steps rather than creating a general goal to "save energy." In this example, an additional ingredient is added to increase the likelihood of people forming an implementation intention: "I pledge to save 10%." A pledge by itself is a commitment technique. The combination of the pledge with concrete steps on how to fulfil the pledge is the basis for an effective implementation intention.

CLEAN   SEPARATE

COOK   CHILL

DON'T LET GOOD FOOD GO BAD.

Check your steps. FoodSafety.gov

In an attempt to prevent food poisoning, the American organisation foodsafety. org started a broad and entertaining programme to make sure that people handle and prepare food in a safe manner. The goal "I will handle and prepare food in a safe manner" is not enough. Thus, specific steps are provided for the food handler to follow: the handler and their materials must be clean; contaminating foods need to be separated from other foods; cooking and serving temperatures are important; and certain foods need to be chilled (and stored) correctly. This campaign attempts to create concrete considerations, such as: "Every time I buy anything capable of poisoning me, I'll follow the clean-separate-cook-chill steps."

WWF uses a simple implementation intention variation in this online ad with a Polar bear: "Click to help." In the image itself, the effect of clicking is visualised. The cursors, necessary to make the saving click, form the essential drifting iceberg that saves the polar bear.

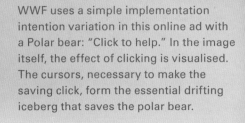

CLICK TO
HELP
ALLFORBEAR.COM

WWF
SAVE
NATURE
TOGETHER

Implementation intentions are part of the broader class of commitment techniques. In all of these techniques, the goal is to transfer an attitude into behaviour by conscious commitment. Although implementation intentions are theoretically a special class of commitment, in real life there is a continuum of how specifically the action will be planned. For instance, planning how the action will be performed can range from a simple commitment ("Yes") to specifying the exact time and place for the activity ("I'll go to my gym at 5 pm this afternoon").

One of the biggest problems in advertising is making sure that people will not only like your product, but will also buy it. Ads can persuade and seduce us with the most beautiful pictures, people, and promises while seeing these ads, but it is likely that these positive attitudes will dissipate or be forgotten over time. When we can get people to make an implementation intention while looking at an ad, it increases the chance that they'll plan and execute their intention to buy later (when the ad is out of sight/mind).

The big challenge here is how to get people to form these intentions via a one-directional form, such as an advertisement. Possible techniques are power and authority ("Plan where and when you'll buy this product, now") or by asking questions ("When and where will you buy this?"). If the ad succeeds in stimulating people to think about the specific actions of the purchase, the chances of success are greatly increased. Implementation intentions are often used in a digital environment (e.g., search, find, choose, and pay) because the actual (buying) behaviour is just a few clicks away and can be controlled and guided more easily.

FINAL REMARKS
→ People overestimate the power of having general goals. The concrete implementation of these goals is necessary.
→ The big challenge is to get people to actively think about how they will execute the behaviour.
→ Implementation intentions work especially well for behaviours related to health, sustainability, and safety.

🔎 **Commitment, Self-persuasion**

23

EFFECTIVENESS | X-FACTOR | IMPLEMENTATION
★★★☆☆ | ★★★★☆ | ★★☆☆☆

RECIPROCITY

Receiving a gift creates the social obligation to return it

Here is a common supermarket situation: a friendly shop assistant offers you a food sample. Automatically, you accept it, and subsequently you feel obliged to purchase the product. Why?

We purchase products in scenarios such as that described due to our inherent need to reciprocate after receiving. Reciprocation is one of the most fundamental human social rules: we feel compelled to return favours. By returning the favour, we preserve the "give and take" balance expected from any healthy social relationship. The technique's effectiveness is partly due to the independence of size between the reciprocal behaviour from the initial favour. In particular, a small gift often leads to a disproportionally large need to reciprocate.

Reciprocity works due to social norms – rules that were imprinted from when we were young about how we treat others in our society. Because of this, returning a favour has become a symbol of building mutual under-standing and trust. Gift-giving is a useful approach to building a lasting customer-retailer relationship. Examples of low-effort symbolic gifts with a high chance of return are smiling, nodding in agreement, and a friendly touch. Low-effort tangible gifts include pins, pens, post-its, etc. These low-effort gifts are suitable for building initial rapport, but do not necessarily lead to a return favour. To ensure reciprocity, it is important that the target feels the initial gift or favour is of high enough value or cost to the giver.

FREE

Free samples are yet another well-known application of the reciprocity technique. They can take on almost any possible appearance: a free newspaper, a free sample of anti-dandruff shampoo in a magazine, a lottery giving you a free first ticket, a first free issue of a magazine, or (as is described above) a free small portion of olives in the supermarket. Of course, one of the main goals is to make people experience the benefits of the product in the hope that they will think: "Wow, these olives taste nice! I'll buy 10 jars." The additional effect lies in reciprocity: They have given me something for free, now I need to show that I appreciate it by doing something in return."

There are many examples of reciprocity, but the most famous and most cited one is probably the, "I'll give you a flower, then ask you to make a donation" approach used by Hari Krishna followers. It is important to note that reciprocity is different from reward. Reward would mean, "If you give us a donation, we will give you this flower." The crux is about who takes the initiative of giving; whereby with reciprocity, the influencer always starts. By the way, in 1999 the US Supreme Court prohibited this kind of soliciting in airports.

Reciprocity can, but does not necessarily, work by increased liking of the giver. A classic experiment by Dennis Reagan showed that after receiving a cheap soft drink from a researcher, people bought twice as many raffle tickets from him later. The reported degree to which they liked the researcher did not influence how many tickets participants bought; rather, ticket purchases were influenced by the level of commitment they felt to return the favour. Importantly, the amount spent on raffle tickets was higher overall than the value of the gifted soft drink. This effect is found in almost all reciprocity experiments, demonstrating that the gain from the return is larger than the cost of the original gift.

FINAL REMARKS

→ The gift should be presented upfront, rather than at the end of a sale.

→ A gift can be anything: coupons, bonus points, special discounts, or something exclusive.

→ The more people feel that the gift is a personal favour from the giver, the bigger the return.

→ A giver must be trustworthy and authentic, without showing the expectation of a return.

→ Reciprocity can backfire: any negative actions are likely to be reciprocated even more fiercely!

🔍 **Dictator & ultimatum game, Game theory, Social norms**

EFFECTIVENESS | X-FACTOR | IMPLEMENTATION
★★★☆☆ | ★★★☆☆ | ★★★★★

GOD TERMS

Some words are so intrinsically good, it is hard to say 'no' to them

Martin Luther King was an absolute master in rhetoric, speeches, and inspiration. One thing he did often was to use words that conveyed either strong positive or strong negative feelings. This made his statements even more powerful, and so hard to disagree with. In many of his speeches, key terms were "equality," "freedom," and "justice." These are terms that all humans value, and pairing these words with his ideas and beliefs increased the attractiveness and moral value of them. Who could disagree with something that promotes equality? Why would you be opposed to an action that will result in freedom? In a similar vein, opposing thoughts and people can be characterised by terms, such as "vicious," "evil," and "hateful." Who would want to be part of the "evil people?" Why would you support something "hateful?"

God terms are words that imply ultimate positive and "good" things. The inventor of God terms, Richard M. Weaver, used examples such as "progress" and "democracy." On the other hand, devil terms are words that imply negative and bad things, such as "terrorist," "deterioration," and "inequality." In politics, war, advertising, and other forms of rivalry, one side will claim moral superiority by describing their own deeds in terms of God terms, while describing those of others (maybe even the same deeds) using devil terms.

With Danone Danio's slogan 'Taste life. To the full', eating creamy yogurt is elevated to a lifestyle. The words 'taste', 'life' and 'to the full' are God terms that respond to our desires and needs to get everything out of life. They are clearly linked to the norms and values of today: life is achievable, you have to be fully yourself and walk your own path. If you opt for something, you go all out for it, like the model in the advertisement: not just a skimpy beard, but a whopper.

Scaling it down a little, many words have inherent positive or negative connotations. Mostly because they refer to the desires, needs, and fears that humans have. For instance, you can sell a detergent because it cleans well or you can say that it promotes health and safety. The latter terms carry more positive feelings and are linked to the universal human need for safety. Any words that strongly activate a need or fear can be used as God or devil terms.

Some examples are:
+ Friendship, love, connect, support (need to belong)
+ Healthy, protect, defend, guard (need for safety)
+ Smart, beautiful, attractive, competent (need for esteem)
+ Freedom, choice, worth, individual (need for autonomy)

God terms and devil terms are used very often in advertising. It is one of the core tasks of the copywriters in advertising agencies to think of the most potent words to deliver a product, brand, and its attributes. In essence, this technique relies on a form of conditioning. A word with intrinsic qualities is paired with your product or brand, thereby strengthening the representation of that brand.

FINAL REMARKS
→ God terms and devil terms play into our needs. Using these words triggers the respective needs in the target.
→ When certain God terms are popular for a while, the power of their use deteriorates.

🔍 **Doublespeak, Promised Land**

Freedom
IS A RIGHT
INDEPENDENCE
IS A CHOICE
JACK DANIEL'S
OLD
No 7
BRAND

HAPPY MAGIC
LOVE
AMAZING
HEALTHY UNITY HOPE
CLEVER CONTROL
NEW
DISCOVER SAVE
WONDERFUL
BETTER STRENGTH SOUL
PASSION JOY
POWER TRUST
BIG WINNER
PEACE

This word cloud consists of only God terms. It is a treat for our brains to read such nice, strong, and positive words. If a brand was attached to this word cloud, it would go straight for world domination.

This ad by the iconic brand Jack Daniels is a fine example of the use of God terms. The short statement: "Freedom is a right, independence is a choice" contains a whopping proportion of God terms (four out of eight) and conveys a high philosophical and motivational quality. Freedom, right, independence, and choice are all words that everyone likes and aspires to. When you read and understand this message, it may give you the feeling of a life-lesson. But what is actually being said here? How will buying/drinking Jack Daniels help you to improve your life?

"

Asked about the power of advertising in research surveys, most agree that it works, but not on them.

ERIC CLARK
journalist and author

25

EFFECTIVENESS	X-FACTOR	IMPLEMENTATION
★ ★ ★ ☆ ☆	★ ★ ★ ☆ ☆	★ ★ ★ ★ ☆

SEX

Does sex sell?

We cannot get around the use of sex in advertising. It is by far the most frequently used and obvious device employed to promote products. Since the early 80s, the use of sex in ads has continued to increase. In 2003, about 50% of all ads included some level of sexual insinuation. There is no reason to assume this will decrease in the future.

Let's be clear about this: Sexual imagery does draw the most attention of any stimuli, hands down. What is less clear, however, is whether the product in the sexually suggestive ad also sells more. While one would expect to find copious amounts of research on this topic, it is surprising to see a lack thereof; in fact, there has been a recent decline in such studies. This may be because scientists generally wish to pursue more "respectable" lines of research. Strangely, of the studies that do exist, most have only employed measures of attention and product memory; few have measured purchasing intentions and almost none have measured buying behaviour. As such, the evidence for its usefulness is mixed. A few pros and cons about this technique's use have been identified, however.

First, sex in advertising is a double-edged sword. It does draw attention, but the attention is directed towards the sexual imagery itself (ALSO SEE HUMOUR, PAGE 67). This means that while sexually laden ads do get more attention than other ads, recall for the product is usually lower. The sexual elements actually draw attention away from the product.

The sexual association is quickly made by the viewer. It feels exciting and attracts attention, but how sensual can some sour, thick, and cold milk on your body be? By the way it's not the milk that is being advertised here! Old Khaki is a South African fashion brand.

Implying sex with vegetables. Why not?!
In the 'Glide' ad, promoting razors for
young men, we just see a banana, an
aubergine, and a zucchini. The slogan
"Most young women prefer clean shaven
men" frames the fruit and vegetables
into a sexual context. The claim "Most
young women..." also manifests a social
proof, putting greater pressure onmen
to have clean-shaven and well-
groomed genitalia.

MOST YOUNG
WOMEN
PREFER
CLEAN SHAVEN
MEN

GLIDE™

RAZOR FOR YOUNG MEN

* Source: DM

Second, while men's evaluations of an ad go up with increasing explicitness of sexual suggestions, women's opinions of sex in advertising appears to be curvilinear, meaning they show higher ad evaluations at medium explicitness, but low ad evaluations at high explicitness. Third, there has been a marked increase in resistance to sexism in adverts, which makes the use of sex risky.

Finally, sex seems to work mainly when the product advertised is directly related to an increase in perceived attractiveness or sexuality. So, when considering whether or not to use sex to advertise, it should be made very clear to the consumer that buying and using this product will result in the sexiness portrayed. Again, note that these results are based almost exclusively on attention, direct evaluation, and recall; not real buying behaviour. As with many of the other techniques discussed in this book, when using sex as an unrelated aspect of the product, this technique could work provided people are in a peripheral processing mode (i.e., not motivated to scrutinise the message). That is, when people carefully process a message employing this technique, they will understand it has been used for attention grabbing purposes only, and subsequent backlash effects can be expected.

Overall, sex in advertising cannot be expected to – and will not – magically increase sales. Additionally, standing out with sex is difficult due to its widespread use. To stand out, one often needs to insert excessively explicit imagery, which then often crosses over into "shock advertising" (with all its possible negative side effects). Thus, ethical issues and public reactions also need to be considered when employing this technique.

FINAL REMARKS

→ The product needs to be directly related to the sexually suggestive imagery.

→ It can be used to attract attention, increase arousal, and momentary positive evaluations (for men).

→ Effects on purchasing behaviour are contested.

𝒪 **Attractiveness, Humour**

EFFECTIVENESS | X-FACTOR | IMPLEMENTATION
★★★☆☆ | ★★★☆☆ | ★★★☆☆

AUTHORITY

People or symbols that signify legitimate authority trigger compliance and obedience

Authority refers to the perceived social position an individual or organisation has in a society, or the recognised expertise someone has in an area of academic knowledge or professional context. In general, authority can apply to one's power and influence over another of inferior rank, stature, age, position, experience, gender, or ability. In some advertisements, celebrities are used to extol a product or service. While celebrities don't possess any authority in a traditional sense, they are admired by the world's citizens, and therefore possess social status.

From a young age we learn that it is wise to listen to our parents, and throughout our lives we learn that it pays to take advice from people who have more experience and more knowledge than ourselves. Unfortunately, this useful heuristic can have unexpected side effects. We automatically defer to anybody whom we believe to be a credible source, and a vast number of studies have now proven our sensitivity to experts and authority figures. (Influence guru Robert Cialdini even claims that authority is one of the six universal weapons of influence).

This innate trust is often tapped into by commercial agencies. By flaunting impressive educational titles, lab coats, business suits, or trustworthy public figures, agencies try to sell everything from toothpaste (recommended by 9 out of 10 dentists), dishwashing detergent

Symbols of authority, like models in white overalls with a name tag and clip-on pen, are often used in washing powder and cleaning product advertisements. The title "the number one choice for the Netherlands" and the authoritarian "number one choice" stamp with the raised thumb are also used as proof of quality, even though it is unclear on what research these claims are based.

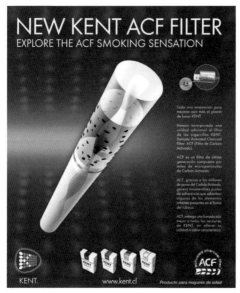

The presentation of a pseudo-scientific infographic also imparts authority. Here a professional digital 3D rendering immediately imparts a sense of truth. The abbreviated name itself ACF (Activated Charcoal Filter) makes it sound more scientific and is further supported by words like "innovacion" (innovation) and "filtro de ultima generacion" (latest generation filter).

A celebrity like Leonardo di Caprio also conveys authority and credibility. Celebrities get their status by popular consensus and media attention rather than from diplomas or expertise. Unlike the examples of doctors and scientists as authority figures – who rarely represent real people – celebrities receive power by representing him- or herself along with their values and personal characteristics.

A PARTNERSHIP TO
HELP PROTECT OUR PLANET

Leonardo DiCaprio and TAG Heuer have joined forces to contribute to Green Cross International initiatives. To learn more please visit www.tagheuer.com

TAGHeuer
SWISS AVANT-GARDE SINCE 1860

He's one of the busiest men in town. While his door may say *Office Hours 2 to 4*, he's actually on call 24 hours a day.

The doctor is a scientist, a diplomat, and a friendly sympathetic human being all in one, no matter how long and hard his schedule.

According to a recent Nationwide survey:

MORE DOCTORS SMOKE CAMELS THAN ANY OTHER CIGARETTE

DOCTORS in every branch of medicine—113,597 in all—were queried in this nationwide study of cigarette preference. Three leading research organizations made the survey. The gist of the query was—What cigarette do you smoke, Doctor?

The brand named most was Camel!

The rich, full flavor and cool mildness of Camel's superb blend of costlier tobaccos seem to have the same appeal to the smoking tastes of doctors as to millions of other smokers. If you are a Camel smoker, this preference among doctors will hardly surprise you. If you're not—well, try Camels now.

CAMEL TURKISH & DOMESTIC BLEND CIGARETTES — CHOICE QUALITY

Your "T-Zone" Will Tell You...

T for Taste ...
T for Throat ...
that's your proving ground for any cigarette. See if Camels don't suit your "T-Zone" to a "T."

R. J. Reynolds Tobacco Company Winston-Salem, N. C.

CAMELS *Costlier Tobaccos*

In the post-war society, smoking ads often used people who conveyed some level of authority. Sergeants, scientists, educators, and even doctors were depicted as satisfied smokers, claiming that it was good and tasteful. And if a doctor smokes it must be safe, right?! The Camel ad presents an idealised physician – wise, noble, and caring.

(lab-tested by "scientists" in white lab coats), and coffee machines (recommended by the famous hollywood connoisseur). All ad agencies know about our unconscious trust in figures of authority, and thus they manipulate symbols of authority to trigger this trust in order to sell their products – even when the authority figure is illegitimate.

Although people consciously believe that authority techniques are outdated, for the unconscious mind authority is just as influential now as it was decades ago. The only reason this approach has fallen from grace is because it's no longer popular – nowadays, people like to feel autonomous, or that they are "free" to make their own decisions.

FINAL REMARKS

→ A fit between the message and the authority figure used is essential.

→ When applied incorrectly, the use of authority can lead to resistance or even the opposite behaviour due to rebellion.

→ Subtle visual stimuli suggesting status, expertise, and authority can trigger the authority heuristic effectively.

🔎 **Agency, Milgram experiment, Moral disengagement, Stanford prison experiment, Ultimate terms**

| EFFECTIVENESS | X-FACTOR | IMPLEMENTATION |
| ★★★☆☆ | ★★★☆☆ | ★★★☆☆ |

LOSS VS GAIN FRAMING

Should the glass be half full or half empty? Fearing loss increases risk-taking; expecting gains increases safety behaviour

Is it best to emphasise the possible gains to be made or what losses can be avoided when advertising a specific product? This question about loss vs. gain framing has been thoroughly investigated by Kahneman and Tversky, two of the most famous researchers in the area of human decision-making. A classic experiment is best able to demonstrate the problem: People were presented with a treatment scenario for a deadly disease affecting 600 people. They were given a scenario that was either positively framed or one with a negative frame. They then had to choose either Treatment option A or B.

FRAMING CONDITIONS	TREATMENT A	TREATMENT B
Positive, emphasising gain	*"Saves 200 lives"*	*"A 33% chance of saving all 600 people, 66% possibility of saving no one"*
Negative, emphasising loss	*"400 people will die"*	*"A 33% chance that no people will die, 66% probability that all 600 will die"*

YOU DON'T SMOKE THE CIGARETTE.

IT'S THE CIGARETTE THAT SMOKES YOU.

SOCIATION
R SMOKER
ARENESS

DESF

Campaigns promoting
healthier lifestyles are often
framed in a negative way.
They tell us that by regularly
performing problem behaviours
we will get ill or even die.
This ad is formulated using
a loss frame. The text tells us:
"You don't smoke the cigarette;
the cigarette smokes you."

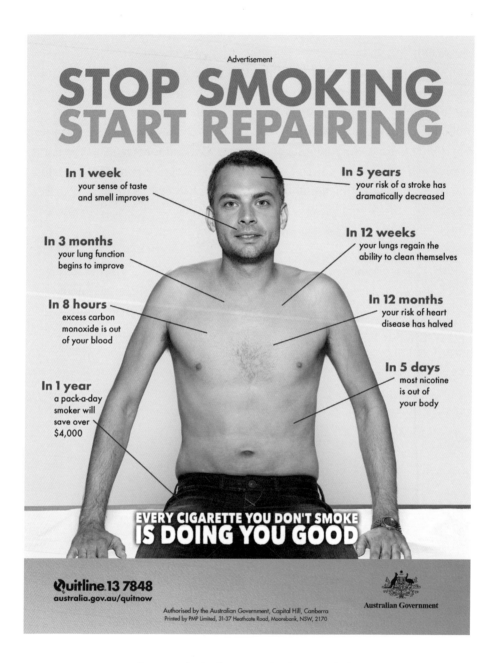

Conversely, in the campaign image of "Stop smoking, start repairing" the message is phrased in terms of the gains that can be made by quitting. It lists the positive effects of not smoking over time, from 8 hours to 12 months after your last cigarette.

More than 70% of people chose Treatment A when it was presented with the positive frame, but more than 75% chose Treatment B when it was presented with a negative frame. The important finding is that people opt for safety if a message is positively framed (Treatment B implies a high chance of losing everyone), but take their chances when it is presented negatively (sure death sounds awful, Treatment B at least makes it possible to save everyone). The options are of course identical (saving 200 or losing 400 from a total of 600), the only difference is the valence framing. These effects have been replicated ad nauseam, demonstrating a fundamental human cognitive bias: we are driven by our emotions, which bypass logical analysis.

Advertisers (who understand this bias) frame messages either negatively or positively depending on whether the desired behaviour should be risk-taking or risk-aversion, respectively. For example, if an expensive purchase or investment has to be made, such as buying a house or stocks, a positive focus on the gains will be beneficial. However, if one wants people to choose the status quo or to opt for damage control, such as voting for a conservation bill or making sure they pay their fines and tuition fees, a focus on loss would be best.

FINAL REMARKS

→ The effectiveness of loss or gain framing is dependent on conscious processing of the message.

→ Just as with fear appeals, a loss or gain frame needs to be followed up by a clear "how-to" instruction to move a person to act (SEE IMPLEMENTATION INTENTIONS, PAGE 126).

→ Everything else being equal, people prefer safe over risky alternatives. This is called the 'certainty effect'.

→ People are, however, more sensitive to feelings of loss than to feelings of gain, and when in a loss situation will do everything to avoid it.

🔍 **Prospect theory, Regulatory fit, Reinforcement theory, Status quo bias**

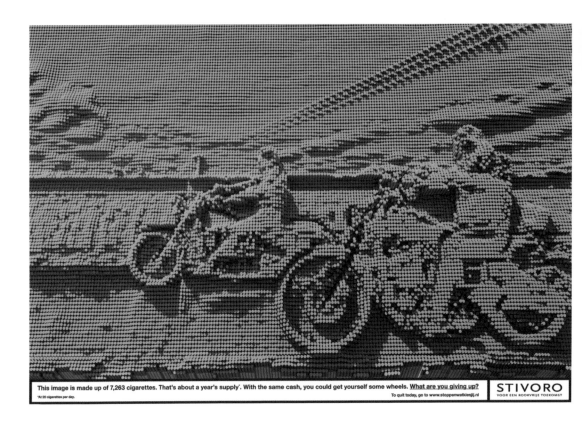

This image is made up of 7,263 cigarettes. That's about a year's supply'. With the same cash, you could get yourself some wheels. <u>What are you giving up?</u>

'At 20 cigarettes per day.

To quit today, go to www.stoppenwatkiesjij.nl

STIVORO
VOOR EEN ROOKVRIJE TOEKOMST

The campaign shows the financial benefits of becoming a non-smoker. It illustrates what you could buy for the money you would save each year by not smoking. Interestingly, anti-smoking campaigns often employ a loss frame. However, a gain-frame approach could be more effective, as it doesn't provoke as much reactance towards the message (cf. loss-framed messages).

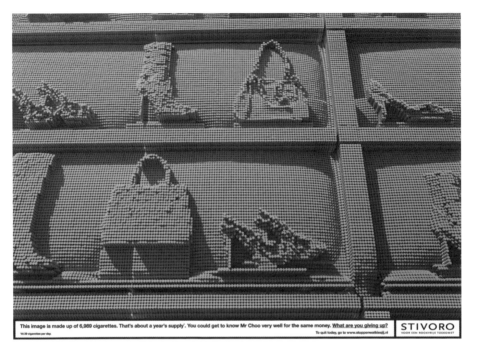

This image is made up of 6,989 cigarettes. That's about a year's supply*. You could get to know Mr Choo very well for the same money. <u>What are you giving up?</u>

*At 20 cigarettes per day.

To quit today, go to www.stoppenwatkiesjij.nl

STIVORO
VOOR EEN ROOKVRIJE TOEKOMST

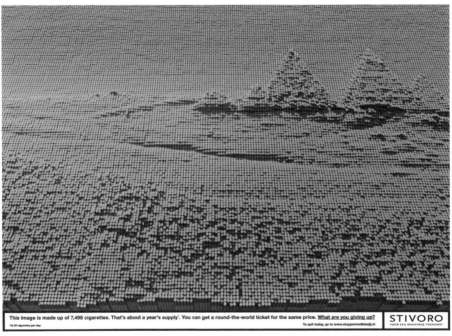

This image is made up of 7,498 cigarettes. That's about a year's supply*. You can get a round-the-world ticket for the same price. <u>What are you giving up?</u>

*At 20 cigarettes per day.

To quit today, go to www.stoppenwatkiesjij.nl

STIVORO
VOOR EEN ROOKVRIJE TOEKOMST

EFFECTIVENESS | X-FACTOR | IMPLEMENTATION
★★★☆☆ | ★★★☆☆ | ★★☆☆☆

RECENCY & PRIMACY

Placing a message at the start or end of a block
of information increases the memory retention
and persuadability of the message

This purely cognitive phenomenon, also known as the serial position effect, is easily described. When people are more convinced by information which is presented first, this is called the primacy effect. When people are more convinced by information presented last, we are referring to the recency effect. What the effects are and that they often occur is clear. However, why they happen, which one is more prevalent, and the exact conditions under which the effects occur is less well-known.

The first reported observations of the effects were related to memory recall, where words and numbers presented at the start and end of a longer sequence were more likely to be remembered. Subsequent research demonstrated that these effects were also true for advertisements and commercials.

A basic explanation for these phenomena is that information presented first only competes with the information that follows (retroactive inhibition), while information presented last only competes with the information presented before it (proactive inhibition). Information presented in the middle, however, has to compete with information presented both before and after it in order to be retained.

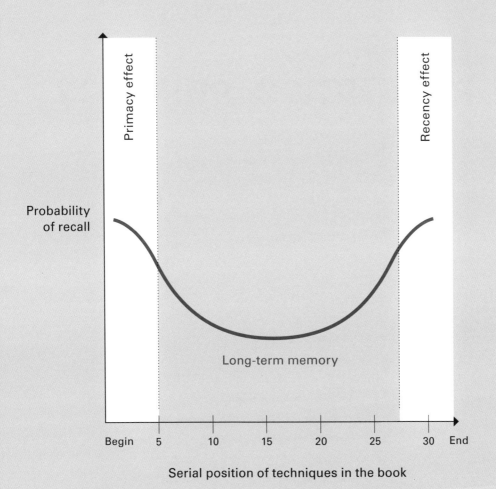

Serial position of techniques in the book

This is a visual representation of how, everything else being equal, the techniques in this book will impress themselves on your memory. The closer the technique is to the beginning or end of the book, the higher the probability you'll remember it. If you end up only remembering acknowledging resistance and subliminals, it means that you probably just scanned the book from beginning to end without much involvement (you've missed out on some good parts in the middle though!).

Are the primacy and recency effects equally strong? It seems that when motivation to process the information is high, primacy takes the lead. The information encountered first sets the bar, and subsequent information is modified or discounted to match the audience's expectations based on this information. Conversely, it has been shown that the recency effect is stronger when motivation to process the information is low, there is a high volume of information, or when the information is presented fast. In these situations, the information is not deemed very important or easy to discern, so what is heard most recently (i.e., last) is easiest to recall and has the greatest influence. This demonstrates the importance of the position of an advertisement when deciding whether to place an ad first or last in a block (i.e., on TV or in a magazine).

One way of employing both primacy and recency effects simultaneously is by having a short "product teaser" campaign, where great expectations are created by only highlighting the positive aspects of the products. The middle part of the campaign could then consist of more extensive, but boring, information about the product. This "normal" product information is normally more sensitive to scrutiny, but will now be filtered positively through the impression created by the primacy effect (i.e., the product teaser). Finally, when the product is about to launch or when purchasing options open up, a final reminder message could be given, which is spiced with more peripheral cues (e.g., using authority and reciprocity techniques), and provide attractive packaging or surprise extras. This reminder message reactivates the product in memory and the positive, but less closely scrutinised, recency aspects add to the primacy effect. This process is often how new smartphones are marketed. Unfortunately, the size of the primacy and recency effects varies widely, making it difficult to predict its impact in advance. A large study using TV commercials found an increase in memory recall and persuasive outcomes ranging from 1% to 30% for information presented first and last. In some countries it is possible to buy the sequence position of the commercial (i.e., within a block) for a set price. Calculations based on context factors such as time of day, message content and importance, size of the commercial block, and viewers' motivation to process the information are needed to determine the cost/benefit ratio of placing an advertisement or message first, last, or in the middle of the block. The take-home message: First impressions last and last impressions stick!

FINAL REMARKS	→ If you are free to choose: Go first if people will pay attention or last if they won't.

          ○ **Attention-decrement hypothesis, Inconsistency discounting, Sleeper effect, Serial position effect**

EFFECTIVENESS	X-FACTOR	IMPLEMENTATION
★ ★ ★ ☆ ☆	★ ★ ☆ ☆ ☆	★ ★ ★ ★ ☆

FEAR APPEALS

Inciting fear to achieve submission and compliance

Fear is a primal emotion associated with the ancient structures of the brain. Throughout evolution, fear has effectively protected our species from deadly threats in the environment. The (un)conscious recognition of a threat leads to a motivation to confront or flee it, a processes known as the fight-or-flight response.

In advertising, the use of fear appeals is found mostly in social marketing campaigns (e.g., to discourage dangerous behaviours, such as smoking, reckless driving, unsafe sex, alcohol abuse, etc.). Generally, the outcome of the harmful behaviour is portrayed by emphasising its physical or psychological dangers. Slogans or additional textual information direct the target to the solution to the threat (e.g., "Stop smoking now!"). Vivid, personalised language often emphasises the similarity between the victim portrayed and the viewer of the campaign, making it harder for the target to avoid or ignore the message ("Young college students like you are 90% more likely to die by...").

While fear appeals are widely used in governmental or social marketing campaigns, research has shown the technique to be flawed. Fear appeals that are too intense can either make the "flight" reaction active in the target group (leading to message avoidance) or can "freeze" or "paralyse" them (impairing further processing of the message).

This is a classic example of a fear appeal. You don't (want to) know where your hands have been and what they've touched. All of these objects could be full of bacteria. In the case of Dettol, it is not necessary to explain how you can avoid the fear; just showing the brand and the product is enough to make people realise that dirty hands can be sanitised using Dettol. There is a strong match between the evoked fear (dirty) and the main brand attribute (hygienic).

Equally problematic for fear appeals is people's need to feel good; they do not like being confronted with negatively framed messages intended to scare them into action. The classic example is the smoking fear appeal in the form of warning labels on cigarette packs (e.g., "Smokers die younger"). In neuroimaging studies, these messages have been found to actually activate wanting and reward areas in the brain, as they have become associated with the smoking behaviour itself. Paradoxically, then, using fear appeals to stop people smoking could lead to more smoking.

For the fear appeal to work, it is crucial to provide a clear and simple, preferably step-by-step, instruction on how to solve or avoid the threat (SEE IMPLEMENTATION INTENTIONS, PAGE 126) rather than presenting the threat alone. Pragmatically presenting the solution to avoiding the threat will increase an individual's feelings of empowerment. Fear appeals work better when the solution is simple (e.g., "Wash your hands" (against infections) or "Stop at a red traffic light" (to avoid death). Research indicates that high self-efficacy, the belief in your ability to perform the recommended response (e.g., to quit smoking), and the certainty that this self-protective behaviour can prevent the threat effectively ("I believe that stopping smoking prevents lung cancer") are the prime predictors for the effectiveness of fear appeals.

In conclusion, using fear appeals is a risky endeavour. A fear appeal is only effective when the threat is experienced as serious and personally relevant, and when the recipient feels a high level of self-efficacy and believes that the new behaviour will be effective in avoiding or reducing the threat.

FINAL REMARKS

→ Increase self-efficacy by identifying behavioural barriers for the recipient and addressing these directly in the message.

→ Always include a solution after the fear appeal, and keep this instruction as simple to achieve as possible.

→ Do not shock, as this could lead to behavioural paralysis and the dismissal of any information that follows the threat/shock.

→ Fear appeals in commercial messages unrelated to health are considered ethically unacceptable.

○ **Emotional seesaw, Extended parallel process model, Shock ads**

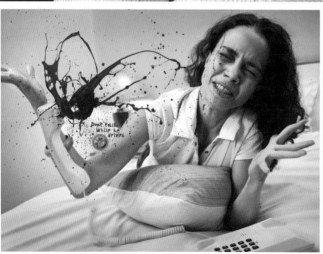

The "Don't talk while he drives" campaign may appear like a typical fear appeal, but it's slightly more advanced. The fear element is obvious: when a driver uses a cellphone while driving, he may be involved in a terrible blood splattering accident. Additionally, however, there is an implicit altercasting element. If you are a good wife, you don't want to endanger your man by calling him while he is driving. A lot of calls made while driving are between partners, so this is an intriguing approach that not only targets drivers, but also who calls them.

EFFECTIVENESS | X-FACTOR | IMPLEMENTATION
★ ★ ★ ☆ ☆ | ★ ★ ☆ ☆ ☆ | ★ ★ ★ ☆ ☆

DOUBLESPEAK

> "War is peace! Freedom is slavery! Ignorance is strength!"
> **George Orwell**

As the one-liner suggests, the doublespeak technique relies on using words that have the opposite meaning to what is true, or greatly distorts the words to give them a more positive connotation. It is the deliberate obfuscation of information, which manipulates people's perceptions of reality to fit the source's purpose.

People have innate negative responses to threatening words (like war, killing and taxes). Describing these words more positively reduces their emotional threat and causes the message (and its source) to be perceived as more tasteful and sensitive e.g., replacing the above with operation freedom, servicing the target and revenue enhancement, respectively. Understanding that we often react on our gut feelings rather than on logic, advertisers and politicians have good reason to twist the truth to their ends. An environment filled with "sugar-coated" terms creates the illusion of a safe and friendly society promising us a rosy future – this takes our focus away from what is important and frees us up to focus on fun things like shopping.

Doublespeak is used for several purposes, for example:
+ Claiming incredible, fantastic, and near-magic product effects
+ Being politically correct to not offend out-groups
+ Saving face by framing failure as good news

UNLOCK A NEW WORLD OF FRESH SMOKING PLEASURE

Start fresh – Stay fresh with L&M

Smoke after smoke your taste stays fresh!

A difference you can taste –
A difference you can feel!

Moisturizing is the secret ... the modern advance in the care of fine tobaccos that seals in natural freshness and flavor. Your taste stays fresher – L&M's *are never drying to your taste.* And you get L&M's famous Miracle Tip – the modern filter that delivers the cleanest, freshest taste possible. So start fresh with L&M today.

Springtime!
It happens every Salem
Salem

Newport smokes fresher!
fresher than any other menthol cigarette
Fine White Filter · Menthol and Mint · Great Tasting Tobacco
NEWPORT

THE MIRACLE TIP

L&M
FILTERS
LIGGETT & MYERS TOBACCO CO.

Start fresh... and keep smiling with fresh L&M.

©1961 Liggett & Myers Tobacco Company

TRY FRESH-TASTING, BEST-TASTING L&M TODAY— PACK OR BOX

Cigarette advertising has always been successful in obfuscating and manipulating people's perception of reality. By combining words like "springtime" and "freshness" with pictures of happy loving couples smoking and enjoying themselves in natural surroundings, the illusion is raised that smoking is healthy! Smoking even affects your taste positively.

The question is: Do we want to live in this seemingly safe, but fake, world or the real one? The answer may not be as clear as expected. We have already, unknowingly, accepted a broad array of doublespeak into our lives. Many of our daily words describe things more positively than they, in fact, are. It has even been argued that using indoctrinating language is the essence of a democratic society. To illustrate: In a totalitarian state, there is dictatorial control over people, so what individuals think is of little consequence; however, in a democratic society, people cannot be manipulated by force, only by words and feelings. Doublespeak is efficient because it's hard to pin down the terms as lies – the interpretation of words is, to a large extent, a subjective experience. It's lying with poetic skill!

Cigarettes can even prevent obesity. Furthermore it protects your throat, fights the irritation, and even works against coughing.

The ultimate goal of doublespeak is to lead to doublethink (coined in Orwell's dystopian book, 1984), where targeted people believe lies to not only be true, but to also be positive and necessary. The big problem with using doublespeak as a persuasive technique is that it pretends to communicate true information. In the short term, this may change people's attitudes and have them buy products, but in the end the illusion will falter. Thus, any resources that have been wasted to generate this illusion could have been put to better use.

Prime platforms to observe where facts are shaped into alternate realities are news channels Fox News and MBNC. The former frames interviews and film fragments in flagrantly right-wing views, while the latter does the same for the left wing.

Doublespeak is a manipulative technique that uses lies and distorts facts. One cannot endorse its use, but we hope readers will now better recognise it.

FINAL REMARKS

→ Extremely unethical!

→ Doublespeak is often so ingrained in our daily language that we do not even detect it.

→ Doublespeak terms often change as people habituate to them.

🔎 **Business speak, Euphemisms, Gobbledygook (sic), Jargon, Propaganda**

EFFECTIVENESS | X-FACTOR | IMPLEMENTATION
★★ ☆ ☆ ☆ | ★★★★ ☆ | ★★★ ☆ ☆

PROJECTION

You look better when you accuse another of your own mistakes

Imagine there were two stallholders at a local fish market and neither sells the freshest fish there. In front of potential customers, one accuses the other of selling old fish. What would the effect on sales be? Projection as an influence technique is commonly referred to as: "The pot calling the kettle black;" we accuse others of our own wrongdoings. The effect of this technique is that the accuser is better liked and the accused gets the blame. Trying to counter the accusation with the same statement ("No, you are the one who sells old fish") does not sound believable.

The broader term, psychological projection, dates all the way back to Sigmund Freud. He described projection as a defense mechanism: We project our own wrongdoings, faults, fears, and other negative elements onto others, and by doing so, we deny that we possess these unwanted elements ourselves. Freud thought it was an unconscious process designed to prevent our conscious mind from having to deal with our own negative "ingredients."

Despite the fact that we can – and will – also project positive attributes, this influence technique involves negative accusations only. That is, a person enhances his own reputation by accusing others of his own faults. Projection works in situations where it is unclear who's the "good" guy and

You are too sweet!

You only care about money!

Unfortunately, no single brand allowed us to use their ads containing projection, thereby illustrating the dubious ethicality of this technique. For examples, just google 'x versus y competitive ad', substitute 'x' and 'y' by big brands in areas such as soft drinks, fast foods, sports and computers.

who's the "bad" guy. The underlying reason for its effectiveness is still somewhat unclear, but most likely several elements are involved, as described below.

For the accused, it is unfortunate that humans automatically tend to believe the information they receive and that it takes elaboration (conscious time and effort) to "unbelieve" this information (SEE ALSO METAPHORS, PAGE 120). So even if it is wrong, once you are accused of something, the label will stick to you. This technique is often used in politics. Just by questioning the politician about their views on leadership, vision, honesty, and so on, the accused politician will be perceived as less competent. Similarly, there are unwritten rules in communication between individuals, one being that we expect each other to tell the truth. Thus, lying is unexpected and we will not always be on guard to detect it.

For the accuser, it is thought that accusing someone else demonstrates that they are someone with the right norms and virtues – someone who dares to stand up against injustice or dishonesty. This may sound counter-intuitive, but our natural reaction is not to challenge the accuser with "but you also have these faults."

An important boundary condition is that there needs to be ambiguity as to who is to blame. That tension, or uncertainty, is what drives the subsequently enhanced evaluation of the accuser. In cases where it is clear which person is to blame, this technique may backfire. A clearly innocent accuser can be perceived as less positive after his accusation. This is probably because there is no uncertainty in this situation and we implicitly associate blaming someone with being unfriendly and not caring about others.

FINAL REMARKS

→ Projection is an unethical technique.
→ Accusing someone else of your own mistakes takes the blame away from you.
→ If the other is clearly perceived as innocent by others, this technique will obviously backfire.

🔎 **Business speak, Euphemisms, Obfuscation, Propaganda**

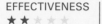

32

EFFECTIVENESS | X-FACTOR | IMPLEMENTATION
★★ ★ ★ ★ | ★★★ ★ ★ | ★★ ★ ★ ★

DOOR-IN-THE-FACE

A large request followed by a small one increases the chance of compliant behaviour

Would you be interested in buying 50 more copies of this book for your friends and family? No? Alright, we understand that that is a bit much to ask. How about just one then?

From increasing donations for charities and cheese purchases in the Swiss Alps to increasing the number of volunteers chaperoning juvenile delinquents at the zoo, the door-in-the-face (DITF) technique has proven to be an effective persuasion strategy. With DITF you can even persuade a stranger to split your bar tab with you! The DITF technique truly is a jack of all trades, but tricky to master. This strategic technique depends, surprisingly, on an initial rejection of the message. By making an unreasonably large first request (e.g., "Could you please lend me €100?") a rejection of the request is guaranteed. Directly hereafter comes a smaller request ("Oh, well, how about €10 then?"). Surprisingly, the chance of success now skyrockets when compared to just asking for the €10 to begin with.

Importantly, the audience has to feel that their initial "No" is a real rejection, and that the second demand is a compromise offered by the requester. This makes the old "give and take" rule active, and one will feel compelled to respond to the compromise. If the first request is too ridiculous, however, ("Can I borrow your car for a year?"), people will dismiss it outright. Conversely, if the initial request is too small,

This US World War II campaign starts with an immense request: To fight! Although most people at that time wanted to help, physically stepping up and joining the army was too much for many. The "or buy bonds" message subsequently plays into any sense of guilt about not wanting to or being able to fight.

SAVE THE WORLD!

START RECYCLING
YOUR PLASTIC BOTTLES
TODAY!

Door-in-the-face is currently a much-used technique for environmental guilt-tripping. Morally, we should all be doing more to save the planet, and we know it! A message like this helps us slightly to buy off our beleaguered consciences. We can't save the planet, but we can at least dispose of our plastic bottles into a recycling bin.

people will not feel the need to compromise on the second, smaller request. The persuasive impact of the DITF is further strengthened by inducing higher feelings of guilt. Saying no to someone can create great uneasiness in the denier, as this is socially undesirable. To reduce this guilt, people will be more inclined to accept the offered compromise as a means to restore the social balance and their peace of mind.

Caution must be advised when implementing this technique, due to its directness. If felt as pushy or aggressive, it may create reactance and possibly even anger in the audience. Such a result would mean a reduced possibility of influencing the audience, including any future attempts at persuasion. Adding a social meta-perspective by emphasising the social situation circumvents possible alarm bells going. For example, after the first request one can state: "This is kind of awkward. There is something else I'd like to ask of you, but tell me if even this seems inappropriate between strangers." This makes it harder to dismiss the situation and plays on the guilt and need for reciprocity already activated in the audience.

Of course, most people would not think of using such a ruse, as it does not fall within social etiquette and is ethically sketchy. This is exactly why the technique is most widespread among salespeople, in aggressive advertising, and by girl scouts going door-to-door selling chocolate chip cookies.

FINAL REMARKS

→ A compromise by the seller makes the buyer feel obliged to reciprocate.

→ Although the technique works with strangers, the closer the requester is to the target socially, the higher the need is for the target to reciprocate.

→ The effectiveness of this technique is maximised when used face-to-face, where it is harder to dismiss the request.

→ Timing is of the essence; the smaller the delay between the first and second request, the better.

🔎 **Ambit claim, Bait and switch, Exchange principle, Reverse psychology**

EFFECTIVENESS	X-FACTOR	IMPLEMENTATION
★ ☆ ☆ ☆ ☆	★ ★ ★ ★ ☆	★ ☆ ☆ ☆ ☆

SUBLIMINALS

Are we mindless machines that are influenced by invisibly flashed images?

Everyone who has seen Fight Club remembers the scene where Tyler Durden (Brad Pitt) splices an image of a large male sexual organ into a children's movie. The result: a theater full of bawling kids. While this was purely for his own mischievous amusement, movies and TV commercials have long been the playground for companies that believe that the subconscious presentation of their products will make people buy them. These subliminal advertisements use super-fast image presentations, hidden shapes, subtle audio suggestions (in radio commercials), or simply use sly word compositions to make certain associations active.

   There is a strong belief that these unconscious presentations steer our consuming behaviour without us being able to curb it. Such beliefs cater to our paranoia about capitalist or governmental conspiracies trying to turn us into obedient consumers, and demonstrate our need to perceive ourselves as autonomous, rational agents. In fact, we dislike this idea even more than being bombarded with conscious influence attempts. This is surprising, given that consciously processed ads have been shown to have effects on our behaviour that are ten times stronger than unconsciously processed ones.

The fact is that the original and widely publicised proof that innocent people unwittingly bought more Coca Cola after seeing the logo flashed during a movie... was a hoax. James Vicary, the father of subliminal advertising and this reported study, has long since admitted that the results were made up. However, it has proven to be a hard belief to expel. This is partly because subliminal advertising is still used and (so the reasoning goes) if companies choose to use it, it must do something, right?

Although subliminal exposure to words and faces has been shown to subtly affect emotions in laboratory studies and to help people unconsciously learn positions of geometric figures, there is little reason to assume that they can influence consumer behaviour in the real world. A large review in the early 90s (of more than 200 studies) showed no effects of subliminal exposure on product choices or evaluations. In all instances, as mentioned previously, they were inferior to the effects of conscious ads. There have, however, been a few very recent studies that give steam to the debate. These have shown that images of soft drinks can stimulate people to choose one drink over another, but only if they were already thirsty. These findings still need to be confirmed on a larger scale, with more choices available, and in "the real world."

Further reason to avoid using subliminal advertising is that large individual differences in the threshold of what is experienced as "subliminal" have been reported by researchers. So even when displaying a visual message subliminally: some people will be able to detect it consciously; some might only register it unconsciously; and others will not even register it unconsciously. This means that designing effective subliminal messages is particularly hard.

All in all, there is no reliable proof that subliminal advertisements work, and if the advertisement is detected, it will lead to strong reactance. Thus, subliminal image or word insertion is one of the most hyped, but largely ineffective, techniques used in advertising.

THE GORE PRESCRIPTION PLAN:

UREAU

THE GORE PRESCRIPTION PLAN:

DUR

THE GORE PRESCRIPTION PLAN:

RATS

THE GORE PRESCRIPTION PLAN:

A heavily debated attack ad on TV by the American Republican Party on Gore's prescription plan. For a very short moment, the word "RATS" could seen on screen before the statement, of which it was part, "Bureaucrats decide" appeared.

THE GORE PRESCRIPTION PLAN:
BUREAUCRATS DECIDE.

An illustration of the subliminally presented text used in the fake Vicary cinema "experiment." Reportedly, no-one saw the words consciously, but moviegoers bought almost 60% more popcorn.

HUNGRY? EAT POPCORN

FINAL REMARKS

→ Subliminal advertising was banned before it was ever actually used.
→ Several research groups are currently working on the exact boundary conditions of the effect.

🔎 **Backmasking, Priming, Supraliminal stimuli**

"

Advertisements may be evaluated scientifically; they cannot be created scientifically.

JOHN WANAMAKER
marketing pioneer

Authors

Marc Andrews (1978, Cleves, Germany) is a visual strategist, designer and behavioural psychologist. This broad field of work provides him with the tools to translate behavioural change strategies into interventions, services and visual communication, using both online and offline media channels. His focus is on combining scientific insights from behavioural psychology with design thinking methodologies. Marc is a partner at andrews:degen. In addition, he teaches Social Design workshops all over the world at colleges and universities, and coaches young designers during their final project in the Communication and Multimedia Design programme at the Amsterdam University of Applied Sciences.

andrews:degen
andrews:degen is an Amsterdam-based creative agency for visual strategies and design, and develops campaigns, branding and digital products. The goal is to carry out projects with a positive impact on society. Together with BCG, the partners of andrews:degen combine scientific knowledge with design and creativity to develop effective online and offline forms of communication and interventions.
www.andrewsdegen.com

Matthijs van Leeuwen (1980, Sarpsborg, Norway) is a Lecturer in Social Influence and Compliance at the Radboud University in Nijmegen, Coordinator of the Masters Programme in Behavioural Change and Head of Postgraduate Training Course for Behavioural Modification Practitioners. His research and education focuses on long-term change through techniques of persuasion and on the questions of how behavioural resistance can be circumvented and how intrinsic motivation can be stimulated. He is co-founder of BCG and provides inspirational lectures on behavioural resistance and intrinsic motivation for commercial parties and government agencies.

Rick van Baaren (1975, Arnhem) is a Professor of Behavioural Change and Society at the Radboud University in Nijmegen. In addition to that, he is an owner of BCG. He is universally regarded as a leading scientist in the field of social influence. He is particularly known for his work on imitation, mimicry and social evidential value. To date, Rick has given a total of over four hundred lectures and workshops in many countries on topics such as influencing and behavioural change.

BCG

BCG Matthijs van Leeuwen and Rick van Baaren are founders of the Behavior Change Group (BCG). BCG is convinced that there is still a world to win for organisations if they have a better knowledge of how behaviour comes about and how it can be changed. That's why BCG makes organisations self-reliant in the field of behavioural change. The company does this by inspiring, training and helping with the application of knowledge in practice. www.gedragsverandering.nl

References

01
ACKNOWLEDGING RESISTANCE
Carpenter (2013). A meta-analysis of the effectiveness of the "But You Are Free" compliance-gaining technique.
Knowles & Linn (2004). Resistance and persuasion.

02
FLUENCY
Alter & Oppenheimer (2006). Predicting short-term stock fluctuations by using processing fluency.
King & Janiszewski (2011). The sources and consequences of the fluent processing of numbers.
Oppenheimer (2006). Consequences of erudite vernacular utilized irrespective of necessity: Problems with using long words needlessly.
Petrova & Cialdini (2005). Fluency of consumption imagery and the backfire effects of imagery appeals.
Reber, Winkielman, & Schwarz (1998). Effects of perceptual fluency on affective judgments.
Song & Schwarz (2008). Fluency and the detection of misleading questions: Low processing fluency attenuates the moses illusion.
Song & Schwarz (2009). If it's difficult to pronounce, it must be risky.

03
FOOT-IN-THE-DOOR
Burger (1999). The foot-in-the-door compliance procedure: a multiple-process analysis and review.
Freedman & Fraser (1966). Compliance without pressure: The foot-in-the-door technique.
Pascual & Guéguen (2005). Foot-in-the-door and door-in-the-face: A comparative meta-analytic study.

04
PROMISED LAND
Bromberg-Martin, Matsumoto, & Hikosaka (2010). Dopamine in motivational control: Rewarding, aversive, and alerting.
Crisp (1987). Persuasive advertising, autonomy, and the creation of desire.

05
SELF PERSUASION
Aronson (1999). The power of self-persuasion.
Bem (1965). An experimental analysis of self-persuasion.
Müller, van Baaren, Ritter, Woud, Bergmann, Harakeh, Engels, & Dijksterhuis (2009). Tell me why... The influence of self-involvement on short term smoking behaviour.

06
ALTERCASTING
Pratkanis (2000). Altercasting as an influence tactic. In Terry & Hogg (Eds.), attitudes, behaviour and social context: The role of norms and group membership.
Turner, Banas, Rains, Jang, Moore, & Morrison (2010). The effects of altercasting and counterattitudinal behaviour on compliance: A lost letter technique investigation.
Weinstein & Deutschberger (1963). Some dimensions of altercasting.

07
SOCIAL PROOF
Cialdini (2001). Harnessing the science
of persuasion.
Baron, Vandello, & Brunsman (1996).
The forgotten variable in conformity research:
Impact of task importance on social influence.
**Platow, Haslam, Both, Chew, Cuddon,
Goharpey, Maurer, Rosini, Tsekouras,
& Grace** (2005).
It's not funny if they're laughing:
Self-categorization, social influence,
and responses to canned laughter.

08
GUARANTEES
Knowles & Linn (2004). Approach-avoidance
model of persuasion: Alpha and omega
strategies for change.

09
ATTRACTIVENESS
Rhodes (2006). The evolutionary psychology
of facial beauty.
Strick, Holland, & van Knippenberg (2008).
Seductive eyes: Attractiveness and direct
gaze increase desire for associated objects.
Van Leeuwen & Macrae (2004). Is beautiful
always good? Implicit benefits of facial
attractiveness.

10
HUMOUR
Eisend (2009). A meta-analysis of humor
in advertising.
**Strick, Holland, van Baaren, & van Knippen-
berg** (2012). Those who laugh are defenseless:
how humor breaks resistance to influence.
**Strick, Holland, van Baaren, & van Knippen-
berg** (2010). The puzzle of joking: Disentangling
the cognitive and affective components
of humorous distraction.

11
SCARCITY
Cialdini (2001).
Influence: Science and practice.
Eisend (2008). Explaining the impact of
scarcity appeals in advertising - The mediating
role of perceptions of susceptibility.
Sandberg & Conner (2008). Anticipated
regret as an additional predictor in the theory
of planned behaviour: A meta-analysis.

12
FLEETING ATTRACTION
**Burger, Messian, Patel, del Prado,
& Anderson** (2004). What a coincidence!
The effects of incidental similarity on compliance.
**Burger, Soroka, Gonzago, Murphy,
& Somervell** (2001). The effect of fleeting
attraction on compliance to requests.

13
DECOY
Heath & Chatterjee (1995). Asymmetric decoy
effects on lower-quality versus higher-quality
brands: Meta-analytic and experimental
evidence.
Huber, Payne, & Puto (1982). Adding asymmetrically dominated alternatives: Violations
of regularity and the similarity hypothesis.
Pettibone & Wedell (2007). Testing alternative
explanations of phantom decoy effects.

14
THAT'S NOT ALL
Brennan & Bahn (1991). Door-in-the-face,
that's-not-all, and legitimizing a paltry contribution: reciprocity, contrast effect and social
judgment theory explanations.
Burger (1986). Increasing compliance by
improving the deal: The that's-not-all technique.
Burger, Reed, DeCesare, Rauner, & Rozolis
(1999). The effects of initial request size on compliance: More about the that's-not-all technique.

References

15
MERE EXPOSURE
Brooks & Highhouse (2006).
Familiarity breeds ambivalence.
Grimes & Kitchen (2007). Researching mere
exposure effects to advertising: Theoretical
foundations and methodological implications.
Reber, Winkielman, & Schwarz (1998).
Effects of perceptual fluency on affective
judgments.
Zajonc (1968). Attitudinal effects
of mere exposure.

16
ANCHORING
Jacowitz & Kahneman (1995).
Measures of anchoring in estimation tasks.
Strack & Mussweiler (1997). Explaining
the enigmatic anchoring effect:
Mechanisms of selective accessibility.
Tversky & Kahneman (1974). Judgment
under uncertainty: Heuristics and biases.

17
ASTROTURFING
Foresman (2010). PR firm settles with
FTC over alleged app store astroturfing.
Lee (2010). The roots of astroturfing.
Streitfeld (2012). The best book
reviews money can buy.

18
ANTHROPOMORPHISM
Aggarwal & McGill (2012). When brands
seem human, do humans act Like brands?
Automatic behavioural priming effects
of brand anthropomorphism.
Epley, Waytz, & Cacioppo (2007).
On seeing human: A three-factor theory
of anthropomorphism.

19
TRUSTHWORTHINESS
Rule, Krendl, Ivcevic, & Ambady (2013).
Accuracy and consensus in judgments
of trustworthiness from faces:
Behavioural and neural correlates.
Todorov, Baron, & Oosterhof (2008).
Evaluating face trustworthiness: a model
based approach.
Todorov, Said, Engell, & Oosterhof (2008).
Understanding evaluation of faces
on social dimensions.

20
DISRUPT & REFRAME
Davis & Knowles (1999). A disrupt-then-reframe
technique of social influence.
Fennis, Das, & Pruyn (2004). "If you can't dazzle
them with brilliance, baffle them with nonsense":
Extending the impact of the disrupt-then-reframe
technique of social influence.
Santos, Leve, & Pratkanis (1994). Hey buddy,
can you spare seventeen cents? Mindful
persuasion and the pique technique.

21
METAPHORS
Ang & Lim (2006). The influence
of metaphors and product type on brand
personality perceptions and attitudes.
Ottati, Rhoads, & Graesser (1999).
The effect of metaphor on processing style
in a persuasion task: A motivational
resonance model.
Thibodeau & Boroditsky (2011).
Metaphors we think with:
The role of metaphor in reasoning.

22
IMPLEMENTATION INTENTIONS
Bélanger-Gravel, Godin, & Amireault (2013).
A meta-analytic review of the effect of
implementation intentions on physical activity.
Gollwitzer (1999). Implementation intentions:
Strong effects of simple plans.
**Van Koningsbruggen, Stroebe, Papies,
& Aarts** (2011). Implementation intentions
as goal primes: Boosting self-control in tempting
environments.

23
RECIPROCITY
Cialdini (2001). Influence: Science and practice.
**Cialdini, Vincent, Lewis, Catalan, Wheeler,
& Darby** (1975). Reciprocal concessions
procedure for inducing compliance:
The door-in-the-face technique.
Regan (1971). Effects of a favor and liking
on compliance.

24
GOD TERMS
Burke (1945). A grammar of motives.

25
SEX
Reichert (2002). Sex in advertising research:
A review of content, effects, and functions
of sexual information in consumer advertising.
Reichert & Carpenter (2004). An update
on sex in magazine advertising: 1983 to 2003.
Severn, Belch, & Belch (1990). The effects
of sexual and non-sexual advertising appeals
and information level on cognitive processing
and communication effectiveness.

26
AUTHORITY
Blass (1999). The Milgram paradigm after
35 years: Some things we now know about
obedience to authority.
Burger (2009). Replicating Milgram:
Would people still obey today?
Milgram (1974). Obedience to authority:
An experimental view.

27
LOSS VS GAIN FRAMING
Lee & Aaker (2004). Bringing the frame
into focus: The influence of regulatory fit
on processing fluency and persuasion.
**Rothman, Martino, Bedell, Detweiler,
& Salovey (**1999). The systematic influence
of gain- and loss-framed messages on interest
in and use of different types of health behaviour.
Tversky & Kahneman (1985). The framing
of decisions and the psychology of choice.

28
RECENCY & PRIMACY
Crano (1977). Primacy versus recency in
retention of information and opinion change.
Haugtvedt & Wegener (1994). Message order
effects in persuasion: An attitude strength
perspective.
Pieters & Bijmolt (1997). Consumer memory
for television advertising: A field study of dura-
tion, serial position, and competition effects.

29
FEAR APPEALS
De Hoog, Stroebe, & de Wit (2005). The impact
of fear appeals on processing and acceptance
of action recommendations.
Tanner, Hunt, & Eppright (1991).
The protection motivation model:
A normative model of fear appeals.
Witte & Allen (2000). A meta-analysis
of fear appeals: Implications for effective
public health campaigns.

References

30
DOUBLESPEAK
Herman (1992). Beyond hypocrisy: Decoding
the news in an age of propaganda: Including
a doublespeak dictionary for the 1990s.
Lutz (1989). Doublespeak: From 'revenue
enhancement' to 'terminal living':
How government, business, advertisers,
and others use language to deceive you.
Orwell (1949). 1984.

31
PROJECTION
Rucker & Pratkanis (2001). Projection as
an interpersonal influence tactic: The effects
of the pot calling the kettle black.
Rucker & Petty (2003). Effects of accusations
on the accuser: The moderating role
of accuser culpability.

32
DOOR-IN-THE-FACE
**Cialdini, Vincent, Lewis, Catalan, Wheeler,
& Darby** (1975). Reciprocal concessions
procedure for inducing compliance:
The door-in-the-face technique.
Millar (2002). The effectiveness
of the door-in-the-face compliance strategy
on friends and strangers.
Pascual & Guéguen (2005).
Foot-in-the-door and door-in-the-face:
A comparative meta-analytic study.

33
SUBLIMINALS
Pratkanis (1992). The cargo-cult science
of subliminal persuasion.
Trappey (1996). A meta-analysis of consumer
choice and subliminal advertising.
**Verwijmeren, Karremans, Stroebe,
& Wigboldus** (2011). The workings and limits
of subliminal advertising: The role of habits.

Image credits

by HHS and/or CDC of any particular organization, service or product. Any views expressed in the publication do not necessarily reflect the views of HHS and/or CDC.
HEART AND STROKE FOUNDATION OF CANADA. Make health last campaign (print, display creative). Launched market: February 2013.

01
ACKNOWLEDGING RESISTANCE
Hans Brinker Budget Hotel. Now even more noise! Graphic Design: Anthony Burrill, concept: KesselsKramer Amsterdam.

02
FLUENCY
Jazz Guimaraes. Atelier Martino & Jaña and collaborators.
Highways Agency. Image provided courtesy of the Highways Agency.
Odis. Ogilvy & Mather, Chile. Art director: Jaime Bustamante, 3D: La Mano Studio, account director: Eric Krohn Bunting, general creative director: Cesar Agost Carreño.

03
FOOT-IN-THE-DOOR
Photo. Violetkaipa, shutterstock.com.
Board. Kaspri, shutterstock.com.

04
PROMISED LAND
Liberation! Happy women's day, guys. Lowe JHB, in-house image.
New Axe Anarchy for him and for her. BBH creative director: David Kolbusz, Dominic Goldman, BBH creative team: Daniel Schaefer & Szymon Rose, photographer: Jean-Yves LeMoigne, retouching: Gary Meade.

05
SELF PERSUASION
Tips from former smokers. Centers for disease control and prevention, July 2013. Tips From Former Smokers campaign. Use of this image in this publication does not imply an endorsement

06
ALTERCASTING
IG. Agência: Lew'Lara\TBWA, client: iG, product: Delas, account managers: Marcio Oliveira, Ricardo Forli, Guilherme Bernardes e Pedro Paulo Mesquita, media: Luiz Ritton, Fabio Walker e Débora Veloso, planning: Daniel de Tomazo e Tatiana Tsukamoto, creative director: Jaques Lewkowicz, André Laurentino, Manir Fadel e Luciano Lincoln, creative: Bruno Cardoso e David Bessler, art buyer: Giuliano Springhetti e Daniela Picchiai, fotógrafo: Ale Catan, image treatment: Platinum, graffic production: Marcos Pedra, client: Alexander Rocco, Suzana Chibante e Bárbara Stanichi.
Lait d'homme. Agency: Chi & Partners. Client: Wing-co.
Now it's time for a Bavaria. Illustrations: Gina d'Achille, concept: KesselsKramer Amsterdam.

07
SOCIAL PROOF
Elvis. Photo of record sleeve, issued by the recording label RCA Victor.
Luckies. Image from the collection of Stanford University (tobacco.stanford.edu).
Thumbs up and heart icon. Icons from Facebook and Instagram.
Have you also noticed so many Hyundais lately? Open Now.

08
GUARANTEES
Crime Stoppers. Target Marketing & Communications Inc..
Pattex – Everlasting. DDB Tribal Düsseldorf GmbH.
STIHL. Publicis Conseil.

Image credits

09
ATTRACTIVENESS
Cover Photo. Ralf Mitsch.
Face of Tomorrow. Sydney Supercomposite,
Mike Mike, 2003.

10
HUMOUR
Free your dog. Advertising Agency: Prolam
Y&R, Santiago, Chile. Creative director:
Alvaro Becker, art directors: Andres Echeverria,
Christian Costa, copywriter: Tomas Cisternas,
photographer: Patricio Pescetto, illustrator:
Ricardo Salamanca, account manager:
Pancho Cardemil.
Splashdown Waterpark. Client: Splashdown
Waterpark, Tom Oliver, creative director: Ian
Grais and Chris Staples, art director: Nicolas
Quintal, writer: Max May, print producer:
Scott Russell, photographer: Mark Whitehead,
studio artist: Jonathon Cesar, account
manager: Marjolaine Durand.

11
SCARCITY
Illustration. By andrews:degen.
Limited edition. Advertising agency:
Ageisobar, São Paulo, Brazil.

12
FLEETING ATTRACTION
Coca Cola bottles. Photo Ralf Mitsch.
Diesel. 'Be stupid' campaign.

13
DECOY
Illustration paper coffee cup.
iStock.com/AliJiva.

14
THAT'S NOT ALL
Digital photo magazine.
Photo by andrews:degen.
Images knifes. Africa Studio and Aas,
shutterstock.com.

15
MERE EXPOSURE
Logos. Trademarks from Nike, McDonald's,
Apple and H&M.

16
ANCHORING
Cordaid – People in Need.
Saatchi & Saatchi / Leo Burnett.
Oral Health. The Partnership for Healthy
Mouths, Healthy Lives and the Ad Council.

17
ASTROTURFING
Illustration. Based on examples
found on internet.

18
ANTHROPOMORPHISM
Biopark. JANDL, marketing a reklama,
Bratislava, Slovakia. Creative director:
Pavel Fuksa, art director: Matúš Nemcík,
copywriter: Adam Rovný, Illustrator:
Noper, account manager: Martin Janík
Heineken logo. Trademark of Heineken.
Refisal. Creative director: Mauricio Cantillo,
creative copy: Julian Mendoza, art director:
Juan David Ospina, illustrator: Juan David Ospina,
agency: Perez y Villa (Medellin, Colombia).
Vigorplant. Armando Testa S.p.A..
WWF. WWF Denmark Campaign by UncleGrey.
Photo Polar bear: thelearnr@flickr, photo
chimpansee: Shutterstock.

19
TRUSTHWORTHINESS
Truthworthiness face simulations.
Alexander Todorov, Social Cognition and
Social Neuroscience Lab, Princeton University,
Princeton, NJ, USA.

20
DISRUPT & REFRAME
Lung Cancer Alliance Work.
Laughlin Constable, Chicago, USA.
Moms Demand Action. Grey Toronto.
Chief creative officer: Patrick Scissons, art
director: Yusong Zhang, producer: Vikki Kuzmich,
account supervisor: Laura Rovinescu, production
company: Sugino Studio, producer: Sarah Ghe-
riani, producer: Taeko Yamanouchi, retoucher:
Miho Matsuoka, photographer: Eden Robbins
Swiss Life. Leo Burnett Switzerland.

21
METAPHORS
Bye Helmets. Photographer: Fulvio Bonavia,
agency: 1861 United S.r.l..
Sekai. Agency: 9mm Propaganda LTDA.,
photography: Alexandre Crespo,
shutterstock.com.
Where does your rubbish go? Photographer:
Andreas Smetana, client: Keep Australia
beautiful, agency: Clemenger BBDO Sydney.

22
IMPLEMENTATION INTENTIONS
Allforbear.com. WWF Russia: Anastasia Lykina,
Maria Vinokurova, Alexander Evgrafov, Victor
Nikiforov. BBDO Russia Group: Creative director:
Nikolay Megvelidze, copywriter: Evgeniy
Shinyaev, art director: Mikhail Tkachenko,
account team: Ekaterina Guvakova, Vladlena
Obukhova, Viktoria Semikasheva, Ekaterina
Chistova, Urnova Maria.
Food Safety. The U.S. department of agriculture,
the centers for disease control and prevention,
the U.S. food and drug administration and
the Ad Council.
**How to destroy Canada's ancient boreal
forest in three steps.** Greenpeace.
Switch off, unplug. Campaign for the city of
Durban, eThekwini municipality, South Africa.

23
RECIPROCITY
Photo Newspapers. iStock.com/AliJiva.
Hari Krishna. Ken Wolter, shutterstock.com.

24
GOD TERMS
Jack Daniel's. The Jack Daniel's advertisement
appears courtesy of Jack Daniel's Properties,
Inc.. Jack Daniel's is a registered trademark of
Jack Daniel's Properties, Inc.. Artwork created
by Helms Workshop.
'Man with a beard'. ©Danone Nederland B.V.

25
SEX
Old Khaki. Agency: Foxp2 Advertising, creative
directors: Justin Gromes & Andrew Whitehouse.
Razor for young men. Agency: BEI Confluence,
New Delhi, India. Advertiser: Glide, brand: Glide
Razor, art director: Sonu Chandra, copywriter:
Manish Ranjan, photography: Nitesh Chakravarti,
client servicing: Vineet Singh, media: Print
(poster), industry: Health & beauty, language:
English, headline and copy text: Most young
women prefer clean shaven men.

26
AUTHORITY
Sun. Agency: Alfred ,creatives:
Aad Kuijper & Patrick de Zeeuw.
Kent. Image from the collection of Stanford
University (tobacco.stanford.edu).
More Doctors smoke Camels. Image from
the collection of Stanford University (tobacco.
stanford.edu).
TAG Heuer. Client: Tag Heuer. Leonardo
DiCaprio is since 2009 the ambassador
of the Switch luxury watchmaker TAG Heuer.
Together they support the environmental
organizations Green Cross International
and NRDC.

Image credits

27
LOSS VS GAIN FRAMING
Adesf. Campaign created by NEOGAMA/
BBH for Adesf.
Stivoro. Client: Stivoro, creative director:
Tom Ormes, copywriter: Tom Ormes,
Axel van Weel, art director: Glenn Doherty,
retouching company: Magic Group.
Stop smoking, start repairing.
Commonwealth of Australia acting through
the Australian national preventive health
agency.

28
RECENCY & PRIMACY
Illustration. Chart based
on the serial-position effect.

29
FEAR APPEALS
Dettol. Produced for Reckitt Benckiser
by Havas Worldwide (2008).
Don't talk while he drives.
DDB Mudra Bangaluru.

30
DOUBLESPEAK
Newport. Salem. Lucky Strike.
All images from the collection of Stanford
University (tobacco.stanford.edu).

31
PROJECTION
Cans. iStock.com/VikiVector.

32
DOOR-IN-THE-FACE
Fight or buy bonds. Image courtesy
of Documenting the American South,
The University of North Carolina at
Chapel Hill Libraries.
Illustration. By andrews:degen,
photo: istock.com/Picsfive.

33
SUBLIMINALS
Bush campaign video. Screenshots taken
from 'You Tube' (search for: Bush campaign
'rats' subliminal message).

Recommended reading

An additional selection of interesting books
relating to persuasion, psychology, advertising,
communication, design, rhetoric and semiotics.

Barthes (1972). Mythologies.

Berger (1972). Ways of seeing.

Cairo (2013). The functional art: An introduction
to information graphics and visualization.

Carnegie (1998). How to win friends &
influence people.

Cialdini (2008). Influence: Science and practice.

Cialdini (2017). Pre-Suasion.

De Bono (1999). Six thinking hats.

Niedderer, Clune & Ludden (2017).
Design for Behaviour Change.

Dorst (2015). Frame Innovation.

Eyal (2014). Hooked.

Fennis & Strobe (2010). The psychology of advertising.

Gass & Seiter (2013). Persuasion: Social influence and compliance gaining.

Hall (2012). This means this, this means that.

Hill & Helmers (2004). Defining visual rhetorics.

Johnson (2012). Problem? Solved!

Joost & Scheuermann (2008). Design als Rhetorik.

Klaus Sachs-Hombach (HRSG.) (2005). Bildwissenschaft: Zwischen Reflexion und Anwendung.

Kress & Leeuwen (2006). Reading images: The grammar of visual design.

Leborg (2006). Visual grammar.

Lidwell, Holden, & Butler (2003). Universal principles of design.

Lieberman (2011). Get anyone to do anything: Never feel powerless again - with psychological secrets to control and influence every situation.

McLuhan (1967). The medium is the massage.

Norman (2002). The Design of everyday things.

Messaris (1997). Visual persuasion: The role of images in advertising.

O'Shaughnessy (2003). Persuasion in advertising.

Packard (1957). The hidden persuaders.

Perloff (2010). The Dynamics of Persuasion: Communication and attitudes in the 21st Century.

Pratkanis (2007). The science of social influence: Advances and future progress.

Pratkanis & Aronson (2001). Age of propaganda: The everyday use and abuse of persuasion.

Reichert & Lambiase (2002). Sex in Advertising - Perspectives on the erotic appeal.

Rose (2007). Visual methodologies: An introduction to the interpretation of visual materials.

Underhill (2008). Why we buy: The science of shopping.

Weinschenk (2011). 100 things every designer needs to know about people.

Williamson (1978). Decoding advertisements: Ideology and meaning in advertising.

Special thanks to all the helpful agencies, brands and organisations who allowed us to use their beautiful im .gery and last but not least, thanks to our family, friends and loved ones.